IN PRAISE OF *LIVING AND DYING*

"As great as all Lifton's books . . . I will put it on my list of recommended readings for those who attend my workshops."

—Elisabeth Kubler Ross,
author of *On Death and Dying*

"They [Lifton and Olson] have presented life's most ineluctable mystery with dignity, simplicity, cogency and even humor . . . Their book for vibrant spirits, searching . . . for the meaning of the death mask is brilliant."

—*Los Angeles Times Calendar*

"Robert Jay Lifton and Eric Olson have produced one of those monumental usable and reusable, readable and re-readable works which promises to produce major shifts in all thinking and teaching about the care of the dying. Somewhere between a hornbook and a *vade mecum,* this book is an absolute must."

—*Omega*

Living and Dying

by Robert Jay Lifton
and Eric Olson

RLI: $\dfrac{\text{VLM 11 (VLR 9–11)}}{\text{IL 9–adult}}$

LIVING AND DYING

*A Bantam Book / published by arrangement with
Praeger Publishers, Inc.*

PRINTING HISTORY

*Praeger edition published August 1974
2nd printing .... January 1975
Bantam edition / December 1975*

Bantam Books are published by Bantam Books, Inc. Its trademark, consisting of the words "Bantam Books" and the portrayal of a bantam, is registered in the United States Patent Office and in other countries. Marca Registrada. Bantam Books, Inc., 666 Fifth Avenue, New York, New York 10019.

PRINTED IN THE UNITED STATES OF AMERICA

For Karen Lifton and
Charles Hall Wicks

Contents

Preface

As I write it is early September, still very warm on Cape Cod. Looking out from the corner of my study window, through the morning mist, I can barely make out the ocean in the distance. A few days ago Eric Olson and I completed our final revisions on this book. (How long have we been working on it? Many years? A few days?)

The mist evaporates, and the dunes and ocean become vivid. They are reassuring in their boundlessness and seeming permanence. The book, on the other hand, is all too vulnerable. (Who will read it? What will they make of it?) Not only vulnerable but perishable. (Will it last beyond this printing? Can it have meaning, over time, for the two people to whom it is dedicated—Eric's grandfather, age eighty-eight, and my daughter, age eight?) Can the book, that is, become in some way part of the endless cultural tide that parallels what the ocean seems to suggest? Can it contribute to this perpetual creation and re-creation of images and forms, even if absorbed and divested of its own original form?

Authors must be permitted such thoughts, especially while writing about mortality and continuity (still more so when authors live by the ocean)—but they should not be permitted to go on this way for too long. So I have developed an antidote for "grand visions," or rather, encouraged such an antidote to pop out regularly from somewhere inside of me. It consists of odd little birds that say odd little things, creatures that have inhabited me almost as long as I can remember and that emerge to express not so much an artistic need (I describe them as a little more than a doodle and a little less than a talent) as my sense of the absurd truth that lies beneath just about everything. Eric Olson and I thought it a good idea to make use of these creatures to introduce each chapter. (Are these guys serious? Won't they be mocking their own enterprise?), and our editor, Mary Louise Birmingham, was courageous or foolhardy enough to agree.

The truth is that the birds *will* mock what we write —will in fact mock the subject of death itself, which I believe to be the ultimate source of mockery per se. Kurt Vonnegut once said, "You can't be funny unless you get close to death, to fear." Turning that around I would say that you can't get "close" to death and elemental fear without becoming a little "funny" in the process. Or, as John Cage put it, no doubt paraphrasing an Oriental sage, "Talking about death, we begin laughing."

Eric and I did have our moments of laughter in preparing this manuscript. (What were we laughing at?) Actually it was he who did most of the preparing, but on the basis of my writings, both published and unpublished. In bringing to bear his own sensibility upon my work, however, he recast it and made his own contributions, especially on the subject of adolescence. I went over all drafts and did considerable rewriting as Eric and I made our final revisions together. The result, therefore, must be viewed as a genuine if idiosyncratic collaboration.

The book makes no pretense of being either a "comprehensive study" of death or a completely "balanced" enterprise in which "this" receives no more emphasis than "that." Nor is it a clinical study of "the dying patient." Rather it lays stress upon holocaust and transformation (the two related preoccupations of my work) and examines more general issues of living and dying from a perspective I have been evolving around the psychological "model," or "paradigm," of death and the continuity of life. Beyond that it will have to speak for itself.

This is my first extensive effort at literary collaboration. I found it demanding and often difficult. But I look back on the work Eric Olson and I did together with a warm sense of our fidelity to each other and to the project. And if a "senior author" might be permitted a final word about his collaborator, I would like to say that Eric Olson's sensitive human qualities and exquisite intelligence illuminated the enterprise from beginning to end.

ROBERT JAY LIFTON

Wellfleet, Massachusetts
September, 1973

acknowledgments

A number of friends who read the manuscript at various stages have helped us make the difficult judgments required by a small book. Among them are John Runyan and David Sloan and their students at Friends Academy; Winnie Barefoot, Jamie Plunkett, Rita Regan, and Charles Vidich; our always helpful editor, Mary Louise Birmingham; and also Betty Jean Lifton. Though we have prepared this book as part of a series for young readers we consider it an essay equally appropriate as an introductory statement of our ideas for our university students and colleagues. Support from the Hazen Foundation and the Harry Frank Guggenheim Foundation made possible much of the work reported in this volume.

1

Death—the Lost Season

The sun she dies so quietly
So sure of resurrection
And I am dying in the street
Crying for connection.
> —TOM RUSH, from the song
> "Starlight"*

And some cease feeling
Even themselves or for themselves.
> —WILFRED OWEN, from the poem
> "Insensibility," in *War Poems*

Historical struggles strongly influence the subjects psychologists choose for study. In our time, massive violence and absurd death have made this century one of horror for millions of people. Death has become unmanageable for our culture, and for us as individuals.

While death has never been fully "manageable" for anyone, death and life are painfully out of joint in our time. In choosing to write a book about death and the continuity of life, we realize we are deeply affected by the present historical situation. What is needed now, we believe, is an approach to death that is both sensitive to personal experience and responsible to broader currents of thought. We would like this book to be a contribution to that insistent human project.

*From "STARLIGHT" by Tom Rush; used with permission.

Seventy years ago, around the turn of the century, sex was more problematic than death as a cultural and psychological dilemma. In 1900 Freud published a book that many people consider the most important of the twentieth century. In that book, *The Interpretation of Dreams,* Freud examined his own dreams and found in their sexual symbolism what he regarded as the deepest sources of human motivation—and the roots of mental disorder.

Freud developed most of his ideas during the late Victorian era. At that time there had as yet been no world wars. The atomic bomb did not yet exist. Science and industry were growing rapidly; people had reason to hope that the fruits of research and economic expansion would solve the world's problems. What people seemed unable to deal with was their own sexuality.

In the Victorian age sexuality was something that polite middle-class people never mentioned. Babies, however, continued to be born, and so we can assume that men and women did have sexual relations. Moreover, the era gave rise to a notably rich pornographic literature. But for much of Victorian society, the less said about such things the better; if one did not think about sex at all, that was better still. The Victorian custom of covering the legs of tables with skirts because of their "similarity" to the human body (no part of which was to be left uncovered) reflects the anxiety, indeed the terror, surrounding sex in many segments of European society at that time.

The patients Freud treated were victims of this social situation. They suffered from anxiety and guilt about their inability to express their sexuality.

4

Sexual impulses repressed by day emerged in dreams at night and in such symptoms as headaches or paralyzed arms. Freud believed that such repression frequently led to disabling psychological conflicts. In working to cure his patients, he emphasized how important it was for them to recognize and accept these sexual feelings.

Much that Freud wrote seventy years ago remains true today. Certainly, people continue to have difficulties with sexual expression. But it is also clear that the times have changed. Rather than ignore sex, we are more likely to flaunt it, experiment with it, or seek new kinds of experience through it. Whatever our relationship to sex, it is no longer taboo.

There is much else that differentiates our time from the era when Freud was writing. We live with the legacy of the atomic bomb and the violent deaths of one hundred million people in this century's wars and death camps. The same high technology employed for this massive killing tends to distance us from virtually all human problems. We are most distanced from the reality of human death. We don't talk about it; we try to conceal, deny, and "bury" it. But—like repressed sexuality in Freud's day—death does not go away. And we too have our symptoms, though they are not the same ones that Freud described.

Death was not always so distant. When people died at home rather than in hospitals, the sight of death was not uncommon. The deaths of grandparents, infants, and mothers giving birth were more frequent. There were no "old people's homes", old and young people lived together in the same house.

Children saw family members and friends die of one ailment or another. The full cycle of life was more visible, and growth, sickness, aging, and death were understood to be part of that cycle. In refusing to face death—as individuals and as a culture—we living today close off a part of life.

Many things have come together now to make death the most central and troubling fact of modern existence. Throughout history, man has feared premature death. The death of a child, a youth, a man or woman in the midst of family rearing and creative work: These images of incomplete, unfulfilled life have always aroused terror. What is new is the awareness that premature death is possible now, not only for an individual man or woman, but for the entire human race. In the past, such apocalyptic visions have been the stuff of nightmares and the prophecy of madmen or religious zealots. That is no longer exclusively the case.

Man is now capable of annihilating himself as a species with his technology. This capacity means that no firm boundary can be drawn anymore between wild fantasy and a sober assessment of real danger. Joyce Maynard, when she was eighteen, wrote about her discovery of the contemporary meaning of death. In her book *Looking Back: A Chronicle of Growing Up Old in the Sixties,* this is what she says:

> People talked about fallout shelters in their basements and one family on our street packed their car to go to the mountains. I couldn't understand that. If everybody was going to die, I certainly didn't want to stick around, with my hair falling out and—later—a plague of thalidomide-type

babies. I wanted to go quickly, with my family. Dying didn't bother me so much—I'd never known anyone who died, and death was unreal, fascinating. (I wanted Dr. Kildare to have more terminal cancer patients and fewer love affairs.)

What bothered me was the business of immortality. Sometimes growing-up concepts germinate slowly, but the full impact of death hit me like a bomb in the night. Not only would my body be gone—that I could take—but I would cease to think. That I would no longer be a participant I had realized before; now I saw that I wouldn't even be an observer. What especially alarmed me about the Bomb (always singular like, later, the Pill) was the possibility of total obliteration. All traces of me would be destroyed. There would be no grave and, if there were, no one left to visit it.

The atomic bomb does not merely destroy; it destroys the boundaries of destruction. With older weapons—an arrow shot from a bow, a bullet from a gun, a bomb dropped from a plane—people are killed or injured, family and community life are upset, but there remains a sense of limits. Some people suffer and die, others recover, and history continues.

The atomic bomb is different. The first atomic bomb used on a human population fell on Hiroshima, Japan, on August 6, 1945. The destruction inflicted by that blast was so nearly total and so longlasting that the survivors of the bomb have experienced a *permanent encounter with death*. No one knows how many people were killed. Estimates vary from 63,000 to 240,000. But even those who survived were left with a devastated city and with fears that their bodies were permanently contaminated from exposure to atomic radiation.

That first atomic bomb was a very small one by today's standards. The world's nuclear arsenal now holds bombs thousands of times more powerful than that one. Such destructive power is not imaginable, not comprehensible. We can contemplate the death of an individual man or woman but not the death of everyone, because we have no images adequate to the possibility of total extinction.

The Vietnam war, like nuclear holocaust, has had a quality of incomprehensibility. Statistics of "kill ratios" and fatalities and even pictures of maimed people have constantly appeared in newspapers and on television. But Americans have not been convinced that all the killing and destruction are necessary. Returning Vietnam veterans have been looked upon, not as heroic warriors, but rather as the unfortunate agents of a policy of death which no one has understood.

Both Hiroshima and the air war in Vietnam are examples of highly technologized violence. In both cases, the use of massive air power has revealed the destructive capacity of technology and the absurdity of the experience of death in modern warfare: unseen victims suffering and dying without ever having met their opponents.

No American military effort prior to Vietnam has been so strongly condemned as immoral. Without the notion that they were fighting for a noble cause or suffering for a higher good, American soldiers have had great difficulty accepting the risks of fighting in Vietnam. The "I-Feel-Like-I'm-Fixin'-to-Die

Rag" of Country Joe MacDonald became *the* song of the war. Its wildly mocking refrain expresses the sense of absurdity of dying in Vietnam:

> And it's 1, 2, 3, what are we fighting for?
> Don't ask me I don't give a damn
> Next stop is Vietnam
> And it's 5, 6, 7, open up the Pearly Gates
> Well there ain't no time to wonder why
> Whoopee we're all gonna die.*

When killing is absurd—because of either the nature of the weapons or the illegitimacy of the enterprise—death becomes unacceptable. To a degree, any form of dying is perceived as absurd, but to live in the face of inevitable death, man requires a sense that his life has continuity and significance.

While the holocausts of twentieth-century warfare have rendered death absurd, the dislocations of the modern world had already rendered life's meaning problematic. People in advanced industrial culture have become so mobile, so rootless, so cut off from traditional sources of meaning that life appears to hold no certainties or reliable values. All of the institutions which throughout history have organized and given meaning to life—family, religion, government, work—are now in crisis.

We live in a time when people find increasing difficulty in giving significant form to their ideas, aspirations, and lives. The subjective experience of psychological and historical (or "psychohistorical") dislocation is precisely a sense of not having a place.

*From "I-FEEL-LIKE-I'M-FIXIN'-TO-DIE RAG" by Country Joe MacDonald, ® by Tradition Music Co. (BMI).

The Beatles express this in the line "Once there was a way to get back home"*; Tom Rush, in the phrase "crying for connection."†

When a society's values and institutions are seriously questioned, life transitions become anxious and traumatic. What does it mean to face the time of marriage when divorce is so common and alternative living arrangements, such as communes and cohabitation, are so widely explored? What does it mean to choose a vocation when all forms of work, and the idea of work itself, are so severely criticized? What does it mean to grow up when adulthood implies being locked into support of a violent, directionless culture? What does it mean to grow old when old people are isolated, put off by themselves in "homes" or institutions, apart from family and ongoing community? What does it mean to die when science has challenged sacred religious beliefs and in the place of spiritual comfort has left only the "scientific method"?

There was a time when Americans could face the transitions of life, if not with ease, at least with some poise and grace. The confidence and candor of these lines composed by Benjamin Franklin for his gravestone reveal no hesitancy to look squarely at death—and beyond it:

The Body of
B. Franklin Printer,
(Like the cover of an Old Book

*From "GOLDEN SLUMBERS" by Lennon/McCartney; copyright © 1969 Northern Songs Ltd. All rights for the USA, Canada, Mexico and the Philippines controlled by MACLEAN MUSIC, INC. c/o ATV MUSIC GROUP. Used by permission. All Rights Reserved. International copyright secured.
†From "STARLIGHT" by Tom Rush; used with permission.

Its contents torn out
And stript of its Lettering and Gilding)
Lies here, Food for Worms.
But the work shall not be lost;
For it will, (as he believ'd) appear
once more
In a new and more elegant Edition
Revised and Corrected
By the Author.

Such a relaxed wit, made possible by the prevailing belief in resurrection, is rare now. Our lack of meaningful rituals and beliefs makes dying the more desperate and fearsome, and impoverishes life as well.

The tumultuous history of America in the last ten years has intensified the crisis in cultural symbols and values that has been visible since the Industrial Revolution, but whose origins date back to Europe's emergence from the Middle Ages. The assassinations of John Kennedy, Malcolm X, Robert Kennedy, and Martin Luther King gave rise to a feeling that America was without leadership, without direction. The black uprisings and ghetto burnings in cities across the country expressed angry disillusionment as increasing numbers of people came to doubt whether America was capable of extending humane treatment to all citizens. Vietnam and Watergate have brought a sense of bitter mockery to the American dream.

These years have been particularly difficult for young people. Asked to fight in a war they did not believe in but could not stop, struggling to define for themselves and the country a new form of political consciousness, the young have agonized over

11

how to grow up in America. For a brief moment in
1969 it appeared that the music and good vibes of
the Woodstock rock festival would give birth to a
new "Woodstock Nation." But over the course of
less than a year the collapse of that hope was
symbolized by a violent death at the next large festival at Altamont, the drug-related deaths of Jimi
Hendrix, Janis Joplin, and Jim Morrison, and the
students killed at Jackson State and Kent State
universities after the U.S. invasion of Cambodia.
Euphoric visions quickly gave way to despair and,
above all, confusion.

John Lennon expressed all this when he wrote,
"The dream is over, what can I say?"* Without a
cultural context in which life has continuity and
boundaries, death seems premature whenever it
comes. Whatever the age and circumstances, it is
always "untimely." But when individual life appears to lack significance beyond itself, death becomes profoundly threatening, unacceptable.

Death is simply a fact—the inevitable end of biological life. The *acceptability* of death depends upon
the psychological context in which it occurs. Death
has now become unacceptable because it is associated with images of absurd holocaust and annihilation and because our lives have become rootless and
disconnected. A well-known study (done, in part,
by Sigmund Freud's daughter Anna) explored the
responses of children to the bombing and destruction of London during World War II. The children's

encounter with death was mediated and profoundly influenced by the responses of the adults around them. Mothers and children huddled together for shelter in dark cellars as bombs fell. During this time of crisis, some children became extremely terrified and anxious, while others were not greatly alarmed. The children seemed to respond more to the emotional attitudes of their mothers than to the bombing itself. Those children who were fortunate enough to have comforting mothers were themselves likely to remain calm. Children whose mothers were not calm became overwhelmed with fear.

The times in which we now live provide no ready emotional context or system of meaning to render death acceptable. We might compare our situation with that of the children in the World War II study whose mothers were terrified by the bombing and conveyed that anxiety to their children. We, too, lack a meaningful and reassuring emotional context.

How might death and life relate to each other in less troubled times? Ideally, death might be seen as life's final season—as autumn is to the summer green of a forest. In late September and October, when the days become cooler and shorter and the angle of sun light changes slightly, the leaves rapidly begin to change color. They fall quickly, and few are left on the trees by November. Leaves do not cling to the trees when autumn signals a time of change—"The sun she dies so quietly."

It had long been an aspiration of men to experience the ebb and flow of human existence as rhythmically as the passages and changes in the rest of nature. This comparison of the changes in the life of a human being with the seasons of nature is compellingly expressed in the words of Ecclesiastes. In the early 1960's when these verses were put to music in the song "Turn, Turn, Turn," first recorded by Pete Seeger and later in a rock version by the Byrds, many people were surprised to discover that the lyrics are from the Bible:

> For everything there is a season, and a time to every purpose under heaven:
> a time to be born and a time to die;
> a time to plant, and a time to pluck up what is planted;
> a time to kill, and a time to heal;
> a time to break down, and a time to build up;
> a time to weep, and a time to laugh;
> a time to mourn, and a time to dance;
> a time to cast away stones, and a time to gather stones together;
> a time to embrace, and a time to refrain from embracing;
> a time to seek, and a time to lose;
> a time to keep, and a time to cast away;
> a time to rend, and a time to sew;
> a time to keep silence, and a time to speak;
> a time to love, and a time to hate;
> a time for war, and a time for peace.
>
> Ecclesiastes 3:1-8

At the time Pete Seeger put a modified version of these lines to music he had been carrying the Biblical passage around for months on a folded piece of paper in his wallet. They are strong words, and they move us because they suggest something we know to be true but generally avoid confronting.

For most people the process of change—accepting the disappearance of the old and welcoming the arrival of the new—is not as graceful and rhythmical as the change of seasons in nature. In India, the passage of life is perceived in "stages": from student to householder to the wisdom of age. Each time of life has a specified activity that is sanctified by religious tradition. For us in the West, and for many contemporary Indians, the rituals and rites of passage which facilitated these changes in earlier times have been lost along with religious faith. Movement from one stage to another, therefore, becomes accompanied by confusion and anxiety—an occasion for trauma rather than celebration.

In this book, we approach these questions through a focus on the formative (or psychoformative) process—by which we mean the continuous creation and re-creation of images and symbols. We view this process as essential to human mental life. A sense of vitality can proceed only so long as the symbolizing process provides forms and images adequate to guide behavior and render it meaningful.

Twentieth-century holocaust and dislocation have combined to create for modern man a kind of "symbolic gap": Our capacity to interpret experience symbolically has not kept pace with the rapidity of historical change. The systems of symbols through which man has traditionally comprehended the world, and the institutions through which he has been active in it no longer provide comfortable images or channels for life. The family, work, religion, government, military service, educational institutions—all these, and even the sequence of the human life cycle itself, are widely criticized and doubted now. The Vietnam war and the Watergate crisis are representative in this sense of a much wider crisis of all of our cultural forms.

When the psychoformative function is disturbed, man becomes desensitized, numb. This happens when historical events are too large or absurd or terrifying to be given meaningful expression through the culture's available symbols. People feel distant from their own lives: "Some cease feeling/ Even themselves or for themselves."

Numbing is the characteristic psychological problem of our age. Jet pilots who coolly drop bombs on people they never see tend not to feel what goes on at the receiving end. Those of us who watch such bombing on TV undergo a different though not unrelated desensitization. To the extent that numbing entails a blockage of feeling, it resembles death. Life itself (or part of it) becomes deadened. Under extreme conditions numbing takes an extreme form, such as in the death camps of World War II, where men and women were turned into what have been described as walking corpses.

The mind cannot take in or absorb those experiences that cannot be meaningfully symbolized and inwardly re-created. In this way, a certain degree of numbing can operate to protect one from great psychological suffering. When numbing is slowly replaced by full awareness, a traumatic experience may be confronted gradually, rather than all at once. But numbing which goes too far and does not cease implies a permanent incapacity to feel.

The process of accepting the death of a loved person usually involves an initial numbness ("I can't believe it") which gradually gives way to awareness. Survivors are confronted with the psychological task of accepting their loss and continuing to live.

In Western culture, when someone dies there is usually a funeral to which family and friends come to mourn for the deceased. Traditionally, the bereaved family was expected to mourn for a full year, to wear black, and to maintain a somber attitude. Many psychological investigators have emphasized how vital the mourning period is for survivors, how necessary it is for their own psychological health. People rarely mourn for a year any more, but there was considerable psychological wisdom in the tradition prescribing that length of time.

During the course of a year, through the full change of seasons and holidays, a family could gradually come to accept the absence of the dead person. Our memories of people are so closely bound up with memories of the times and places they have shared with us that the process of "remembering that someone has died" takes time. For a child gradually coming to believe that the death of a father is real, the largely unspoken psychological process of mourning would be something like this: "It's summer and Daddy is not here when I go swimming; it's fall and Daddy is not here when we eat Thanksgiving dinner; it's Christmas and Daddy is not here when we open the presents." Slowly a child accepts the repeated evidence of his senses and concludes to himself, "Daddy will not be here with me any more." A similar process takes place for mourners of any age.

The ease with which a child, or anyone else, accepts the death of someone close depends upon many things. Generally, if a child feels part of a loving family and is given emotional support and the chance to express in his own way his sorrows and fears, he will begin again to play and study and carry on his own young life with a minimum of self-pity and self-blame.

For survivors' mourning process, the "grief work" requires an initial loss of feeling which persists until new images and feelings take shape that allow the loss to be accepted. If the mourning process is not carried through, a person may remain inwardly numb indefinitely. In historical times when religion played a larger role, the comfort of a church and belief in God were of great help to people in mourning. For us now, such support is less available; this loss is part of contemporary psychohistorical dislocation.

We attempt to conceal what we can neither face nor escape. The Forest Lawn Memorial Park cemetery in southern California epitomizes our attempt to "bury death." There, at the world's largest cemetery, death itself is a dirty word. The "loved ones" (never referred to as "the dead") are elaborately embalmed, decorated with cosmetics and smiles to appear alive and happy, and then "laid to rest" (not "buried").

Even in hospitals, death is embarrassing and has no place. The doctors and technicians are committed to using their science and equipment to keep people alive—at least to keep them breathing. Death becomes a defeat for medical science, an unwanted intrusion, and is not accepted as a human event that has its place in the seasons of life. As one prominent engineer said, "We will lick the problem of aging completely so that accidents will be the only cause of death."

The most absolute effort to stave off final extinction is the freezing of bodies immediately after death. The dubious rationale behind this "cryonics" movement is the assumption that these bodies can be cured and brought back to life when cures are discovered for the diseases responsible for these deaths. The more common techniques of organ transplantation are now extending the lives of people whose hearts or kidneys no longer function.

Though new medical techniques have brought much relief from suffering, their more extreme manifestations reflect our difficulty in accepting death as part of the life cycle. They then lead us further to deny that there is "a time to be born and a time to die." Dylan Thomas urged his father:

> Do not go gentle into that good night,
> Old age should burn and rave at close of day;
> Rage, rage against the dying of the light.

But rather than raging against the dying light of life, we find ourselves refusing to believe that the light ever dies. We hide from ourselves the very fact of death.

The historian Arnold Toynbee once said that death is un-American. He meant that in a culture that places so much emphasis on progress, strength, and the vitality and beauty of youth, and so little on the wisdom and dignity of age, death has no place. In such a society, dying can be a terribly lonely and desperate experience—as indeed it often is.

The repression of sexuality led to an underground and often perverse fascination with sex known as pornography. Our denial of death has resulted now in movies, books, and magazines which exhibit what the English anthropologist Geoffrey Gorer has called "the pornography of death." Though this kind of pornography includes much exploitation, it also reflects the attempt to create meaningful psychological ideas around death and expose false ones. This development reveals both the persistence of the human tendency to formulate experience and our overwhelming need to confront death honestly.

In agrarian communities of the past, death could not be concealed. Man's earliest villages and cities were in fact built around burial sites for dead ancestors. Hunting and gathering peoples made pilgrimages to the burial places to honor the dead who could no longer travel. Such fixed places eventually became cities. What began as cities for the dead became cities for the living as well.

Modern cities are for the living only. Those who are old or weak or dead have, like obsolete cars, no place in them. But there is a growing sense that the fact of human death can no longer be denied. Psychiatrists are becoming increasingly concerned about patients left amid the tubes and machines of the modern hospital to face death alone. People everywhere are coming to an awareness that man's new capacity to destroy himself requires new thinking about death if we are to comprehend our current historical crisis.

The extremity and danger of the present historical moment suggest that we need the theme of death to reconstitute our lives. In the words of Ecclesiastes, there is "a time to every purpose under heaven." Now is the time to ponder the words of the novelist E. M. Forster: "Death destroys a man; the idea of Death saves him."

2

Death and the Life Cycle

What man shall live and not see death?
                              —Psalms 89:49

So much of adolescence is an ill-defined dying,
An intolerable waiting,
A longing for another place and time,
Another condition.

                              —THEODORE ROETHKE,
                              from "I'm Here"

What can we know of death and how do we know it? Throughout history man has answered this question in many different ways. Is it true that, as Freud said, man cannot imagine his own death, or as La Rochefoucauld put it, "One cannot look directly at either the sun or death"? Erik Erikson, a psychologist well known for his studies of human development, has written that when a person tried to imagine not existing, he experiences a chill and a shudder and turns away. Many religious philosophies, on the other hand, have provided explicit images of life after death, images so attractive that people have longed for an end to earthly existence so as to experience heaven.

We want to understand what kind of knowledge people can have of death. Before proceeding to that controversial problem, we can begin by asking a more basic question about knowledge in general: How do human beings learn? Here also, there are disagreements, but two famous positions are important to consider.

One of the oldest beliefs, held by Plato in the fourth century B.C., is that all knowledge exists within one at birth. What appears to be later learning during the course of life is then really only a remembering of what was once known and then forgotten. The most one could learn before death would equal what was forgotten upon being born.

The seventeenth-century English philosopher John Locke believed the opposite. He argued that a child knows absolutely nothing prior to birth. Because we learn everything from experience, said Locke, there are absolutely no limits on what a person can learn during his life provided he has the right experiences.

Modern psychological evidence now suggests that both Plato and Locke were partly correct. It appears that a child does have a kind of knowledge at birth, but that this "knowledge" is vastly extended and made concrete only by experience with the environment. We shall use the word "imagery" rather than "knowledge" when speaking of what a newborn baby knows about the world. In any case, it seems incorrect to assume, as Locke did, that a baby's mind at birth is absolutely blank.

A newborn baby expects to be fed and "knows" what to do with the mother's breast. The baby's inner imagery guides it toward the mother and helps it to become a partner with the mother in obtaining what is needed to survive. But as the inner image motivates and guides the baby, so also does experience help it to learn specific things. The image gradually begins to resemble a picture of the baby's relation to the world. After about six months, for example, the baby learns that one person is its mother. Once this happens, the baby is most content in the arms of this special person and is less easily comforted by the arms and smiles of others.

Several kinds of evidence have convinced psychologists that a baby's brain is not simply empty at birth. In watching a young baby, we become aware that it has certain innate, or inborn, expectations. Also, recent studies have given us reason to believe that infants react to images while they sleep. What it is that a baby "sees" in these states can never be fully known. But it does seem clear that the capacity to form images is present at birth.

Observations of the behavior of very young animals suggest that some kinds of knowledge are inborn. Certain young birds when they are hungry peck at a dot of color on their mothers' beaks. This is a signal for the mother to open its mouth and provide food. The young bird had to have some inner image or picture of its own relation to the world in order to begin pecking the dot.

In speaking of behavior that is directed solely from within an organism, psychologists have usually used the term "instinct." Freud thought there were two kinds of instincts: those that push the organism (animal or human) toward life and those that tend toward death. Freud saw the process of living as a kind of battle between these life and death instincts. The life instincts urge the organism to satisfy appetites and thus reduce the tension of various kinds of hunger. The death instincts pull the organism back to the inanimate state from which Freud thought all living organisms emerged. Thus, both sets of instincts lead the organism toward inactivity—the death instinct directly and the life instinct through the restful state that follows satiation. And, indeed, Freud said explicitly that "the aim of all life is death."

The problem with the word "instinct" is that it suggests a blind force that always exists in more or less the same form. The term "inner imagery" is more useful because it indicates that these inner guiding pictures are constantly changing throughout the life cycle. The baby is guided by inner imagery toward an attachment with the mother. But this imagery itself changes form and evolves as the mother-child relationship develops during the early years of life. The imagery becomes increasingly complex as the child learns to speak and acquires words with which to think about its place in the world. The term "instinct" conveys an idea of behavior more machine-like and less influenced by language and changing imagery than is appropriate to human action.

The inner imagery exists at first only on the level of physiology. At this point it is not an image at all, in the sense of being an inner picture of the world. Rather, it is simply a predisposition of the organism to move toward the nurturing it requires. Later, during early childhood, this imagery does become something of a crude picture of self and world. The child recognizes familiar faces and objects and becomes content in their presence and anxious in their absence. Later still, with the more complete learning of language, the images become concepts and forms of thought which can be communicated. During this sequence of development, the imagery takes on an ethical quality; it comes to indicate what one *should* do. Thus, inner imagery responds to changes in one's age and life situation; it evolves.

Though we will be speaking here of death *imagery* rather than death *instinct,* there is something important to be learned from what Freud said about the death instinct. He had the idea that death is somehow present in a unified way from the beginning of life. For this reason, death plays a central part in his view of life. But because he spoke of death only in terms of instinct, he underestimated the importance of imagery and language in shaping a person's evolving vision of self and world.

Man's task is to develop concepts, imagery, and symbols adequate to give a sense of significance to his experience. In saying that "the aim of life is death," Freud asserted that there is an instinctual drive toward an inanimate state. Though we now find this instinctual language misleading, we would agree with what we take to be the basic idea behind this assumption: that death is psychologically present from the beginning of life.

A child requires several years to acquire a *concept* of death. This concept is built gradually on the basis of inner imagery that the child apparently has at birth and that is developed and made concrete in relation to the child's experiences. The particular nature of those experiences can profoundly affect the "feel" that the idea of death comes to have for the child. Over the course of the life cycle, the imagery and ideas associated with death continue to evolve, reflecting both individual experiences and development of intellectual capacities.

We can understand the child's earliest imagery of life and death as organized around three sets of opposites:

connection — separation

movement — stasis (lack of movement)

integrity — disintegration

In describing the imagery surrounding the child's relationship to the mother, we spoke of the expectation of food and care. The child seeks attachment to the mother and has an inner image which guides it in this way. The baby cries, sucks, clings, follows, and smiles—trying always to get the care it needs. We can say that life for the baby means being *connected* to the source of care and support. Powerful fears and anxiety appear when the child is left alone, separated from the source of nurture. This image of *separation* is related to an image of death.

Anyone who has watched healthy babies and young children has seen their energetic motion. Muscles and muscle coordination develop with exercise. This is precisely what children seem determined to get by engaging in various kinds of play. *Movement* is life. *Stasis*—the opposite of movement—is associated with imagery of death. When a young child is held still against his will, he becomes nervous and upset. Inability to move is equated with death.

Young children are, of course, least in motion

when they are asleep. And it is interesting that the most widely known of all nighttime prayers begins:

> Now I lay me down to sleep
> I pray the Lord my soul to keep.
> If I should die before I wake,
> I pray the Lord my soul to take.

The popularity of this old prayer reveals its closeness to the psychological equation made by children of sleep and death, and the need for an image of continuity. We would stress the importance of such imagery in the child's life. Later psychological disturbance can often be traced to an early impairment in this imagery of life-continuity.

In some situations this association of sleep with death can make death less frightening. This possibility is shown in an example from the life of a little girl just over three years old, reported by Sylvia Anthony in *The Discovery of Death in Childhood and After:*

> Marlene was brought to school by her father, who had found her lying beside her dead mother on the floor by a half-made bed. The mother had apparently suffered a heart attack. On arrival at school, Marlene said quite happily to the teacher, "Mother lay down on the floor and went to sleep, so I went to sleep too."

Only over time does the child come to be able to differentiate death from sleep and appreciate the finality of death. The preschool child, for example, often thinks that death is reversible, as a "coming back." Later it is recognized that death is not only final, but also inevitable, and that it happens to everyone, including oneself. The age at which children begin to understand all this varies tremendously, but in most cases it occurs between five and nine. It is important, however, to emphasize that children begin to become aware of death much earlier than this, even though their ideas may be vague and confused.

The phrase "getting it together" suggests something of what is meant by the third pair of opposites. The *integrity* of life means staying in one piece, keeping oneself intact. The opposite image is that of *disintegration*—of falling apart and going to pieces. From the earliest days of life, the fear of bodily annihilation and disintegration is strong. This fear is related to fears of separation and stasis, since all death imagery is bound closely together. But we can speak of early fears of disintegration as a threat to one's image of one's body, and of its boundaries as inviolable. Cuts, injuries, the sight of blood—these can generate extraordinary anxiety because of their closeness to the death imagery of disintegration.

Situations that relate to imagery of separation, stasis, and disintegration cause extreme anxiety even when the experiences themselves are not actually dangerous. Imagine a young child wailing and screaming when his father leaves him alone for a moment in a strange place, or the great fears which a small cut and oozing of blood can bring. These exaggerated fears become more understandable if we see them in the context of the more ultimate image of extinction to which they relate.

Otto Rank, an early psychoanalyst, believed that all anxiety in life resulted from life's first great shock: the trauma of being born. At the moment of birth the complete security of the womb is exchanged for the unpredictable stimulation of the world. In this view, birth is such a frightening experience that it creates fears which never again completely vanish.

Instead of saying that birth creates all anxiety, we prefer to say that birth is the first experience to activate the child's innate potential for death imagery. The baby is suddenly separated from its mother, must now move on its own, and is all at once vulnerable to pain and the fear of disintegration. As a baby becomes a young child, then a youth, and passes through maturity to old age, the same process will be experienced again and again. Each new step (each new "birth") on the way to becoming a fully developed person will rekindle the death anxieties associated with the innate imagery of separation, stasis, and disintegration.

This life-death imagery endures and evolves throughout life. The imagery becomes more concrete and specific as the child has experiences of seeing dead animals, severely injured people, or anything that suggests separation, stasis, or disintegration. Certain kinds of extreme experiences can heavily weight the death imagery, as opposed to the life imagery, in a young child's mind and can create lasting problems of anxiety. The death of a young brother or sister may be such an experience. This can convince a child that death happens because you're small.

Sometime around the age of three or four, a child becomes conscious of the concept of death. When death becomes a distinct idea, the imagery of separation, stasis, and disintegration becomes bound together in a unified notion of what it means to be dead. Typically, children think of the dead person as having "gone away" or having been the victim of violence such as biting, shooting, stabbing, bombing, burning, automobile crash, being flushed down the toilet, or having the body burst open so all the blood comes out. The way in which each child understands death will be strongly affected by the kinds of death he has seen or heard discussed. Middle-class children are more likely to think of death as caused by old age or disease, while poor children in inner cities often associate death with violence, accidents, or suicide.

A child's concept of death is likely to be charged with fear when earlier death imagery has overwhelmed imagery of life and continuity. Experiences that reinforce imagery of life's connection, movement, and integrity will encourage an attitude of trust and hope. A child seeks to grasp the idea of death while having the idea of continuity affirmed. This is very different from having the reality of death kept from him.

Such children's games as "hide-and-seek" reflect an early concern with disappearance and return. There is evidence that this concern is present from the first months of life, and that playing "peek-a-boo" is an earlier version of the same game. What seems most important is that the child's early curiosity in this area not be denied or ignored. A parent can use the occasion of a child's finding a dead animal to explain something about death. Or the death of a pet can be mourned, and even a grave marker erected, so as to help convey the idea of death and ongoing life. If ideas about death are not developed gradually in this way and talked about at appropriate moments, the death of a child's friend, brother, sister, or parent can be a trauma from which there will never be full recovery.

A child's early response to death affects the whole of personality development. Relaxed conversations with older people about death can make a vast difference in the way a child absorbs experiences with death. A child may develop guilt and feel responsible for the death of someone close, or think that, because a person he loves dies, it is not safe to love. Being able to discuss such matters openly may help avoid the development of harmful conflict.

Freud tended to see fear of death as secondary to fear of castration, in keeping with his sexual emphasis and his idea that death has no psychic representation. There is no doubt that fear of castration can arouse strong anxiety in young boys. But we would see the fear of death as the more fundamental anxiety, and castration epitomizing this anxiety in a particular body part. There is a further problem with Freud's theory when applied to women, because there is no precise analogy in women to castration fear in men. (Surgical excision of the breast can arouse somewhat similar anxieties in women later in life.) We are critical of the male bias in Freud's theory and of Freud's view of fear of death as subordinate to fear of castration. We should recognize, however, the ways in which—in both sexes—death anxiety can become localized in a specific part of the body.

If the conditions of a person's life suddenly change, death imagery may intensify. At a number of times in the life cycle, there are "critical points" —major transitions that occasion a flare-up of death imagery. When the changes have to do simultaneously with one's own body and with the social world in which one lives, then one may easily lose confidence in the belief that anything is definite or reliable. It's like Bob Dylan's line "How does it feel to be on your own, a complete unknown, like a rolling stone?"* There seems to be neither a comfortable world nor a known self.

The transition from childhood to adulthood is such a time. This period is known as adolescence and usually begins between the ages of twelve and fifteen, with the commencement of puberty. For girls becoming women, the transition is marked by menarche, the beginning of monthly periods of vaginal bleeding. For boys becoming men, the erect and stimulated penis is now capable of discharging semen. Both sexes may experience this new capacity to discharge bodily fluids as fearful and emotionally upsetting. The body that one has lived in for years suddenly appears to be acting unpredictably.

A girl who has not been told in advance about menstrual bleeding can become extremely frightened upon seeing blood on her clothes. If this happens at a social gathering or at school, she may feel embarrassment as well as fear. Not surprisingly, the experience of unexpected bleeding activates imagery of disintegration and thus becomes especially fearful. Girls beginning to menstruate sometimes think they are dying. The idea that one is now ready for sexual intercourse, which for a woman means being penetrated by a male, may also arouse fear.

For boys, too, at adolescence, the body feels out of control. The first ejaculation often occurs at night during a dream, a "wet dream." These dreams are likely to include sexual images which can themselves cause anxiety.

One's body—suddenly growing rapidly, making one awkward, and behaving unexpectedly—seems not quite one's familiar home. But no new safe place appears to replace the lost one. Adolescence has been called a time of storm and siege. Strong sexual fantasies urge intimacy with another person, which is both fearful in itself and socially taboo. New and tougher demands are being made at school, and questions about plans for the future become more pressing. Friends suddenly seem more competitive and are often harsh in their judgments and rejections. In all of this, the search for forms of connection becomes intense and sometimes desperate.

For the first time in life, one consciously confronts the void: It suddenly seems possible that one could be nothing. One appears to rely on a past that seems lost and a future that feels unimaginable.

Where to retreat from all these assaults? It is tempting to play, in fantasy and reality, with the image of oneself as still a child. But it is precisely childhood that has been so suddenly and irredeemably taken away. When one acts like a child, one is laughed at by friends and chided by parents. The past offers no escape. Adolescence itself is a death and rebirth experience; one dies as a child and is reborn as an adult.

All of the threats to the adolescent's self and world increase the anxiety coming from death imagery and intensify the search for new ways of affirming the imagery of life. This imagery now assumes a metaphoric and ethical quality. *Connection* comes to signify not only physical attachments, but also a sense of relation to meaningful philosophies and purposes. *Movement* for the teenager implies more than bodily activity: It includes emotional and intellectual development and a dread of stagnation. The image of *integrity* takes on the connotation of ethical intactness ("getting your head together") as well as soundness of body. Imagery of life must now be affirmed in a way that seems personally "right"—and an adolescent's judgments of his own ethical evasions can be every bit as severe as those he pronounces on others.

Adolescents frequently become extremely critical of their parents and families. This criticism is usually perceived by parents as hostility and rejection—and in a way it is. The hostility does not come entirely from hate, but also from an intense struggle to be independent of one's family and from inner doubts about one's capacity to do so. Above all, adolescence is a state of vulnerability. The emerging adult self feels impossibly frail; parents must often be attacked for the self to assert its vitality and power. Nor has it been sufficiently realized how much an adolescent's devaluing of his family can raise inner questions for himself about his own biologically mediated sense of connection.

There must always be an element of tension in the relationship between generations. But the nature of this relationship is also influenced, like everything else in psychological development, by history and historical change. In a period of rapid change, the wisdom of age has to compete on more even terms with the wisdom of youth. In such a time, the young *do* know more about certain crucial matters than their parents and teachers. Parents and teachers themselves are not so convinced of the adequacy of their own past experience as a basis on which to give advice, and often have real misgivings about their capacity to make judgments about the lives of the young.

All of this puts an element of uncertainty and fluidity into cross-generational relations. Age alone is not sufficient to make one an authority on all issues. The young become teachers of the older generation, and at certain moments of mutual trust, the rigid forms break down. The young still seek the authority of older people, but an authority based on lived experience and knowledge rather than on age alone or hierarchy—an authority which confirms rather than stifles their own emerging perceptions and critical spirit.

The fact that the parents of adolescents are usually in their forties intensifies the problems. Middle age brings its own crisis and another flare-up of the death anxiety which accompanies imagery of separation, stasis, and disintegration. (We will say more later about this mid-life transition.) But it is necessary to understand that the fires of family strife are fueled by crises of continuity and death imagery in the lives of both generations.

Adolescents are frequently described in such contradictory terms as brooding, frantic, lazy, energetic, creative, dull, friendly, spiteful, and so forth. They can be all of these at one time or another, for they find themselves subject to rapid and seemingly unpredictable swings in mood. The stress is on experimentation both in thought and action as the young person now tirelessly tries on new beliefs and stances to determine which, if any, will fit. Our historical period leaves more options open and makes this experimentation both urgent and exciting, and yet terribly difficult. It is precisely because our society needs new images of adulthood so desperately that it is not easy now to become an adult.

Adolescents struggle most to avoid deadness and to seek life. This pursuit can mean an emphasis on energetic creativity, tireless action, or the contemplation of grand visions. The foibles and failings of adult society appear inexcusable. There is much greater awareness of potential than of constraint and limitation; virtually anything seems possible. The young person restlessly seeks modes of continuity and activity that seem justifiable—goals that are worth working or even dying for. Often the beginning plans for a life's work are laid in this time of questioning and search.

One way to view the adolescent period is to see it as a time when a young person enters history. Suddenly that which is most personal—one's sexual feelings and consciousness of mortality—leads one to make connections that are more than personal. Sexual desires impel one toward intimacy with other persons and ultimately make one part of the cycle of generations. Awareness of death leads to questions about the meaning of life, and to a search for ways to relate oneself to the larger human historical project.

Sexuality and death make possible evolutionary change in the species, and in that sense they serve the impersonal natural process. The moment of exhaustion and relaxation after sexual orgasm which the French call *la petit mort* ("the little death") has been interpreted by some to suggest an experiential connection between sex and death. But we would stress the ways in which both sexuality and awareness of mortality lead to the enlargement of the boundaries of the self.

The Catholic theologian John Dunne calls this self-enlargement the making of one's "life story." There are, Dunne says, not only the given biological "events" of one's life, such as sexual maturation and death; there is also an element of leeway in how one chooses to relate oneself to these events. This process of forming meaning around biological universals enables one to have a life story rather than merely a life chronology.

A meditative youth may begin during adolescence to record his activities and feelings in a diary or journal, writing down his own history partly out of the desire to make certain he has one. Adolescent brooding may give rise to a philosophy of life, an idealistic statement of how things might be if adults didn't interfere. From political speculation and the quest for moral authenticity may emerge determined political activity both in school and in the larger community. In view of what we have said about life imagery, it is interesting that the radical politics of youth in the 1960's came to be known as "the Movement."

Not all societies have offered their young what we think of as adolescence. Puberty is biologically universal, but in some cultures this physical change also marks the beginning of adult responsibilities and privileges. In our society, many years intervene between puberty and the entry into full adulthood. This is the long period of schooling which societies with complex technologies require for access to most jobs. Moreover, this in-between time of more-than-child but less-than-adult seems to be growing longer, and the limbo status it creates can make for difficult psychological tensions.

Adolescents sense the precariousness of their own mental state. It is obvious that few things in the young person's life are stable or settled. Disappointments and hurt feelings are both frequent and extremely painful. The question that young people ask with greatest urgency is not "How can one feel?" but rather "How can one keep from feeling so deeply—how can one defend oneself from hurts that are too deep? Can one love while keeping in oneself a secret place that is safe?" There are many approaches to this problem, but no final answers; it is a problem that remains long after adolescence.

To open oneself to love and growth is to become vulnerable also to loss and disillusionment. The problem of attachment is as profound for psychology as it is for religion. Even where there is a quest for total freedom from attachments, as in some forms of Buddhism, one forms an attachment or connection with a great spiritual tradition. Whatever one's choice of attachments, they place one in a position of risk. Freud once said, "Life is impoverished, it loses in interest, when the highest stake in the game of living, life itself, may not be risked," though he did not incorporate this insight into his theory. One can, however, cultivate areas of the self that take on fierce autonomy from attachments to people around one. Such areas of commitment inevitably connect with larger traditions and enduring principles, but even these are not invulnerable.

We would emphasize the need for a sense of connectedness to currents and processes beyond the self if vitality and psychic energy are to be maintained. This is the theme of the next chapter.

Young people sometimes adopt special ways of *appearing*—to themselves and others—to be growing and evolving without exposing themselves to the anxiety of actually facing loss, which is a form of death imagery. One such technique is to become extremely intellectual, to explore new alternatives only in thought or in conversation. In this way one's life may seem to have connection, movement, and integrity, while actual changes and commitments are avoided. Or an adolescent can develop an ascetic style in which he denies his own strong appetites and fantasies and regulates his life with extreme control and discipline. In this way, too, life appears to have movement, while the real risks are avoided.

A third common approach is the retreat to conformity—to being like everyone else. This enables one to feel a sense of connection and shared participation, again without confronting one's own fears and doubts. A teenager in a strong group can appear to be rebelling against adult society while safe with friends who believe exactly as he does. Such youthful cliques gain a sense of power by harshly excluding those who are not "good enough," those who do not fit with themselves. The language which adolescent cliques use, their own forms of slang which change rapidly, is an effective way of defining the boundaries of one's in-group. Adolescent prejudice, stemming as it does from the anxieties aroused by unconfronted death imagery, can be cruel and inflict wounds not soon forgotten.

The quest for continuity *can* arise from a need to compensate for the overwhelming degree of death anxiety the adolescent feels. And the techniques that are used to cope with this anxiety *may* be evasive rather than honest. But the quest is also an affirmative one in which a young person attempts to stake out with integrity his own boundaries in relation to an acceptable world. Defensive and authentically exploratory approaches can be so similar as to be indistinguishable from each other. In any case, the projects of protecting and extending the self go on simultaneously. Overintellectualizing and real play with important ideas, ascetic evasion and the search for honest simplicity and purity, mindless conformity and the painful struggle to find other people worth belonging to—these are the tensions that an adolescent feels as he seeks to define himself as a person.

The struggle to achieve a sense of continuity and significance—to affirm the connection, movement, and integrity of life—becomes intense during adolescence but does not end there. Just as the adolescent searches for an authentic form of adulthood, so adulthood itself is marked by a need to feel that one's life has not stopped and become futile. But while the adolescent son or daughter reels with the dizzy freedom of having all possibilities open to him, his parents in middle age are more likely to be feeling nagging doubts about choices already made and lived with for twenty years. The approaching departure of children in whom so much has been invested means a beginning of separation from an important souce of meaning. By mid-life too it may appear that one's occupational commitment, for better or worse, is final. Does one's life still have any movement and integrity left?

Children reawaken in their parents memories of their own youthful struggles. For most adults, the teenage years are remembered as a time of tension, but at least a time of some freedom and open choices. Thus, when parents see their own children reaching this time of infinite possibility—endless decisions about education, marriage, style of life— they may feel an intensification of regret about their own "roads not taken."

A parent may critically and insistently push his son or daughter toward his own lost chances. In so intruding, he is likely to succeed only in convincing his children that he has no respect for *their* integrity. Certainly, at this time of personal doubt, the last thing a parent wants to hear is endless criticism from adolescent offspring. But as we have seen, this is precisely what adolescents—for their own reasons —are likely to give. In this desire to avoid criticism while dispensing it freely (and in their separate confrontations with death imagery), the two generations closely resemble each other.

The whole issue of the generations becomes even more tense and difficult in a time of psychohistorical dislocation like our own. No institution now seems fully acceptable, no form of work or commitment goes uncriticized, no life-style completely justifiable. What it means now to be an adult in this situation is perplexingly unclear. If adulthood means to be somewhat settled, then one must become numb to constant criticism of whatever settlement one makes. But such numbing is itself a form of deadness, as the young are so capable of pointing out.

Does attaining adulthood require partial deadening? Our answer would be that adulthood does require certain forms of selective numbing. But that numbing need not characterize adult experience itself—and there are widespread experiments in our culture that challenge stereotyped images of adulthood and stress not only openness to feeling, but also a capacity for self-mockery and absurdity so often expressed by the young.

On the life watershed of middle age, one becomes aware that life is not unbounded at the far end. The boundary of one's death is suddenly no more distant than the boundary marked on the other end by one's birth. One is in the middle. Of course, one has always "known" that one would die, but now this knowledge becomes a compelling individual reality. One's life is suddenly felt to be limited, finite. It also becomes apparent that one cannot finish everything; there will not be time for all one's projects.

The apprehension that one's life may not only be finite but also *incomplete* sparks the fears that always accompany thoughts of premature death. For some people, this apprehension leads to a number of negative consequences: resignation and despair, retrenchment around seemingly irrevocable commitments, damning criticism of "hippies" and "bums" who live their lives more playfully. But for others, middle age brings a new birth of energy, a renewal of effort and experimentation.

Certainly, creativity and energy are not properties belonging exclusively to adolescents. However, as one psychoanalyst, Elliot Jacques, has argued, creative energy may express itself somewhat differently by the time one reaches the age of forty. Jacques points to many artists and musicians, for example, whose careers have changed dramatically around middle age. Their mode of work at this stage becomes slower, more careful and painstaking; it assumes a quality Jacques calls "sculpted"—as opposed to the more intense, spontaneous, ready-made quality of work done earlier in life. This change may have to do with a sharper awareness of personal mortality and finitude that comes with middle age.

Adults need movement and experimentation, too, and when they are unable or unwilling to acknowledge this, their lives become constricted. This very constriction of personality can be a way of evading real challenges which cause too much anxiety when confronted. But it is true as well that the burdens of adult responsibility and commitment mean that dramatic change at this time of life is more difficult and fearful. The uncertain gains of trying something new at this stage have to be balanced against the security of known patterns and achievements which one desires to protect.

Perhaps one of the most fortunate consequences

of our restless culture is that more adults are making changes in ideas, work, and other life patterns when they feel themselves caught in dead ends. Ironically, the same confusion and openness of our present historical moment that increase the anxiety of life transitions for some people make experimentation possible for others.

Because our times are characterized by rapid change and scant confidence in the institutions of family, work, and church, personal quest is made both more possible and more problematic. But, however one deals with middle age, the need for a sense of life's continuity becomes more intense. One looks to family ties, commitment to work, the experience of nature or art, or the solace of religion for symbols of enduring and significant life.

A final critical point in the life cycle is that of old age. Death is near, and the aged person has ample time—usually too much time—to ponder what his life has added up to. Though the basic contours of life are set, the struggle for continuity is still very real. The tendency of the old to reminisce represents their need to reassure themselves that their lives have contained integrity, movement, and connection —a pattern which psychiatrists have now formalized in a therapeutic approach called the "life review."

The wisdom of age does not have a large role in the youth-centered culture of America. Far from worshiping our ancestors, as in traditional Asian societies, we shun the old and create separate "homes" in which our "senior citizens" can spend their "declining years." These euphemisms reflect our neglect. It is the old themselves who most painfully experience this culture's avoidance of age and death.

The generations need each other. Old people have not only wisdom to share, but playfulness as well. The fact that many older people are still interested in sexual love (a "discovery" that the mass media have been recently making) simply illustrates this potential for full human communication. Many an adolescent who has found his father or mother "impossible" to talk to has discovered in a grandparent a more flexible attitude. An old person, having less of an investment once more in what society thinks of as conventional, may feel more free to listen to and explore new ideas.

There can be "play" (in the sense of fun as well as leeway) in old age, but only when the old are respected and are part of ongoing communities. If age is denied a meaningful place in the flow of life, death—even for the old—can seem premature. At this time of life, as earlier, the fear of death is heightened by the negative death imagery of separation, stasis, and disintegration. Serenity in the face of death depends upon a sense that, in some symbolic way, one's life will endure.

3

Symbolic Immortality

when you yourself are the embodied continuance
of those who did not live into your time
and others will be (and are) your immortality
*   on earth.*
                                        —JORGE LUIS BORGES

there's time for laughing and there's time for
*   crying—*
for hoping for despair for peace for longing
—a time for growth and a time for dying:
a night for silence and a day for singing

but more than all (as all your more than eyes
tell me) there is a time for timelessness
                                        —E E CUMMINGS, from
                                        #11, *95 Poems*

The idea of immortality is the answer to a profound human question or, really, the answer to two such questions. The first question is, What happens to a person after death? The second is, How can a person live without overwhelming anxiety in the face of the certainty of death? Behind both questions lies the human aspiration to live forever.

It is possible to look at all of human history as a record of man's diverse answers to these questions of immortality. Religions and empires have been founded, wars fought, and untold millions of people killed on behalf of conflicting notions of the path to immortal life. And the concern about immortality,

53

as well as the debate about what it means, continues in our own time.

Freud said that the aim of life is death. By this he meant to convey at least two distinct ideas. The first implication of this concept is the idea of the death instinct as an innate tendency toward return to an inanimate state.

Instincts are modes of energy that lead to certain forms of life-preserving behavior. Therefore, the concept of an instinct that leads to death is something of a contradiction in terms. As we have suggested previously, however, Freud's idea of a death instinct did contain an important element of truth that should be preserved: that death is psychically present from the beginning of life. As explained in Chapter 2, we wish to preserve this Freudian insight about the psychological significance of death. But we believe that this influence of death on psychological life is due to the importance of symbolization in mental activity rather than to what Freud called a death instinct.

What we call experience can occur only insofar as our minds are able to give form to our perceptions. This form structures and orders sensory data. "Seeing" and "recognizing" are thus very closely related, because inner psychic structures create meaning and the possibility for recognition. The inner forms in our minds are images and symbols which can be either very clear and distinct or rather vague and cloudy. The most general psychic organization of these inner images and symbols takes place around the polarities of connection-separation, movement-stasis, and integrity-disintegration. The extreme form of separation, stasis, and disintegration is death, and imagery that relates to these is psychologically extremely powerful.

The second implication of Freud's concept of the death instinct is that "every organism wants to die in its own fashion." In that spirit, recent psychiatric investigators speak of the "appropriate" death, by which they mean a readiness to die because a full life has reached completion. But this sense is often inseparable from despair—the feeling that one no longer has sufficient purpose to go on living.

These problems have been dealt with chiefly in literature, philosophy, and theology—disciplines outside the realm of science. Only recently have psychologists become concerned with them. The scientific world view has generally been limited to questions of the "means" of life, rather than confronting problems of ultimate value. The purposes of human life and the question of what lies beyond it—these are precisely the issues that science has considered inappropriate to its proper concerns. Because science has great prestige in our society, scientists' avoidance of issues of value has a profound influence on our culture and our lives.

Psychology has been partly within the scientific tradition in this sense and partly outside it. Most academic psychologists have been more interested in psychological *mechanisms* (such as how people learn) than in questions of ethical *goals* (such as what it is people should learn). On this point Freud was a great rebel, because he was concerned with alleviating psychological misery. To achieve that end, he believed people should be educated to as cept reality, and he was convinced that the scientific truths discovered by psychology would lead to the abolition of man's spiritual illusions.

Chief among humanity's illusions, in Freud's view, was religion. He saw the spiritual comfort given by religion as a false support used by people who had not outgrown childish dependence on parents. Maturity, according to Freud, would consist in facing squarely the hard realities of life, and death, and not searching after false hopes.

Freud saw the idea of immortality as supreme among civilization's false hopes. He said that this illusion derives from clinging to the pretense that one will not die, and that it serves to compensate for the reality of death which is too hard to accept. Freud believed that by pinning its hopes on an illusion— the illusion that death is not total and final—civilization undermines its only real hope: the rational pursuit of the truth.

When, in his later writings, Freud attacked religion as an illusion, he aroused almost as much controversy and contempt as he had in his earlier emphasis on the importance of sexuality. Freud insisted that death is *final* and means the total annihilation of the organism. He believed that doctrines of the immortality of the soul derive from a childlike refusal to accept the finality of death.

In the early 1900's, Carl Jung, initially one of Freud's followers, began to take psychology in a very different direction. Jung had done extensive study of world religions and mythology and was impressed by the discovery that myths from all parts of the world and in every age have contained beliefs about life after death. Jung felt that the long history of mythology must reveal deep truths about the nature of the human mind that psychology was ignoring. These truths Jung called "archetypes"— universal psychic images which he believed arose from the deepest level of the unconscious. Jung argued that humankind's relatively recent stress upon narrow materialistic science could bring about the loss of the vital truths displayed in dreams and myths. To ignore these universal archetypal truths would result in the impoverishment of psychic life.

Jung described the psychic vitality of "primitive" peoples who live in tune with archetypal truth. And he observed the positive effects of belief in myths for persons nearing death. He said that when man's conscious thinking is in harmony with the deep truths of the unconscious revealed in mythology, then fear of death is no longer overwhelming. Life can then be lived to the fullest until the end. Therefore, Jung, in contrast to Freud, encouraged belief in religious teachings because he thought such belief was, in his words, "hygienic"—necessary for healthy living. He wrote:

> When I live in a house that I know will fall about my head within the next two weeks, all my vital functions will be impaired by this thought, but if, on the contrary, I feel myself to be safe, I can dwell there in a normal comfortable way.

Jung was convinced that the unconscious part of the mind has a timeless quality and that belief in eternal life is consistent with the timelessness of the unconscious. To achieve psychological wholeness, in his view, requires that one become more in touch with this part of the unconscious in daily living. In his autobiography, published posthumously, Jung wrote:

> If we understand and feel that here in this life we already have a link with the infinite, desires and attitudes change.

We can learn something important from both Freud and Jung. But neither, in our opinion, had a totally satisfactory view.

Freud stressed what is biologically true about death: its absolute destruction of the organism. He was also aware of man's great capacity for self-delusion. Though he knew that confronting death could heighten the vitality of living, he did not grasp the symbolic significance of images of immortality. In this he underestimated the human need for images of connection beyond the life span of each individual. This need is not itself delusional, nor need it necessarily result in delusions. Freud was bound to a conception of psychic activity that we think fails to do justice to the characteristically human tendency continually to create and re-create images and inner forms. We speak here of symbolization as a process rather than the creation of specific symbols. What we have referred to as the psychoformative process encompasses this overall tendency, and its complexity is such that it cannot be reduced to the idea of the sexual or death instinct. The important question, then, is how and when symbolization can become rich enough to sustain full vital life.

Here, Jung made a real contribution. He took religious imagery very seriously and appreciated its significance in man's search for meaning and the effort to express it. The problem with Jung's position is that he did not always distinguish between man's need for symbolization around immortality and the literal existence of an afterlife. We agree with Jung that the scientific tradition as reflected in Freud's insistence on seeing religious symbols as mere delusion misses the point of such symbols. But Jung's refusal to distinguish between symbolic meaning and literal reference undermines and distorts both religion and science.

In the seventeenth century, a French philosopher named Blaise Pascal proposed what he called a "wager." If there is no afterlife, and one doesn't believe, then one has lost nothing, Pascal argued. But if there really is such a thing, and one fails to gain admission through lack of belief, then all is lost. Therefore, Pascal argued, since there is everything to be gained by believing, and nothing to lose, one should make the wager and decide to believe in the afterlife. Jung's position is a bit like Pascal's wager. Moreover, Jungian symbols tend to have a fixed quality, so that there is little connection between what Jung calls archetypal symbols and ongoing history.

Our own view of symbolic immortality draws from both Freud and Jung. We would stress not only the finality of death, but also the human need for a sense of historical connection beyond individual life. We spoke in Chapter 2 of the need to develop concepts, imagery, and symbols adequate to give a sense of significance to experience. This psycho logical process of creating meaningful images is at the heart of what we will now call *symbolic immortality*.

We can see the sense of symbolic immortality as reflecting man's relatedness to all that comes before him and all that follows him. This relatedness is expressed in the many kinds of symbolization that enable one to participate in ongoing life without denying the reality of death. Without this unending sense of attachment to aims and principles beyond the self, the everyday formative process we have been discussing—as well as the capacity to feel at home in the world—cannot be sustained. When people believe in such cultural projects and expressions, they feel a sense of attachment to human flow, to both their biology and their history. They feel a *sense of immortality* which enables active, vital life to go on.

This sense of immortality is expressed in five modes or categories: biological, creative, theological, natural, and experiential.

Biological immortality is perhaps the most obvious mode. It means simply that a person lives on through (and in) his sons and daughters and their sons and daughters in an endless chain. In addition to generational continuity, this mode also symbolizes the reproductive cells as they are passed along from parent to child.

The biological mode of immortality has been greatly emphasized in East Asia, especially in China and Japan, where the failure to have offspring implies lack of respect for ancestors. But the idea of a continuing family and a "family name" protected from blemish is important in all cultures. The act of writing a will to insure the transmission of inherited wealth to one's descendants reflects this concern for the preservation of one's posterity.

This mode is never purely biological. It is experienced emotionally and symbolically and transcends one's own biological family to include one's tribe, organization, people, nation, or even species. Similarly, the sense of biological continuity becomes intermingled with cultural continuity as each generation passes along its traditions to the next.

We can speak of a kind of "biosocial immortality" that occurs through the continuity of one's family and other important social groupings. Historically this mode has been a mixed blessing. It has encouraged cooperation with those beyond one's immediate family (one's people), but has also led through chauvinism to the killing of those whom one views as "different." Nevertheless, there has been a significant trend among large numbers of people throughout the world to view all of humanity as a single species sharing a common destiny. Unfortunately, that beginning recognition has hardly touched ideological and nationalistic antagonisms.

A second mode is that of human "works," or the *creative* mode. One may feel a sense of immortality in this mode through teaching, art-making, repairing, construction, writing, healing, inventing, or through lasting influences of any kind on other human beings—influences that one feels can enter into a general human flow beyond the self. In professions like science or art that have a long heritage, one is frequently aware of the historical sources of one's own work and the tradition that one's own contribution is maintaining.

In such service professions as medicine or education, one has a sense that one's direct influence on patients or students is transmitted to more distant persons not seen or known. When efforts at healing or teaching seem unsuccessful, one may feel a profound despair originating in the perception that one's efforts are not making any lasting difference. This despair itself reveals a deep human need to have an enduring effect—to leave a trace.

Ordinarily, when one's work is progressing well, there is little conscious concern with its immortalizing effect. But when the products of creative effort do not seem sufficient to embody one's sense of self, then the question (previously unconscious) of the value and meaning of one's life and work begins to become a conscious concern.

The Christian tradition has distinguished between "work" and "works." "Work" in this sense has referred to mundane, often unsatisfying toil which regenerates neither the worker nor his community. "Works" imply contributions of lasting value to the larger community; these contributions are made in part through one's "vocation."

Entering a vocation was originally dependent upon feeling oneself "called" to do some particular kind of work, and the word vocation still suggests something beyond just a job. It implies that one feels in one's work connections and commitments beyond the self. At some level of consciousness, such actions are perceived to involve the lasting extension of the valued elements of one's own life into the lives of others. Through such doctrines as karma, service, and duty, other religions have expressed similar ideas.

The *theological* mode of immortality is the one most readily suggested by the word immortality. For, historically, it has been through religion and religious institutions that people have most self-consciously expressed the aspiration of conquering death and living forever. Different religions give the assurance of immortality in different ways, but concern with the problem of the meaning of life in the face of death is common to all religious traditions. No religion is based on the premise that human life is eternally *in*significant. Thus, Buddha, Moses, Christ, and Muhammad, through various combinations of moral attainment and revelation, transcended individual death and left behind teachings through which their followers could do the same.

The danger with religious images of immortality is that they can quickly lose their symbolic quality and result in the assertion that people don't really die. For centuries, great religious teachers have attacked institutionalized "religion" as the real stumbling block to authentic spiritual attainment. Such images as heaven, hell, reincarnation, and the resurrection of the body are often understood in the same sense as scientific observations of nature. Thus, the concept of the "immortal soul"—a part of man that escapes death—was seen by Freud as a characteristic example of the human capacity for self-delusion through religion.

We believe Freud was justified in his attack upon literalized doctrines that deny death. But Freud did not appreciate that religious symbols of life after death or life beyond death can mean something other than literal images of angels living serenely in a blissful heaven or, negatively, damned souls condemned to eternal suffering in the fires of hell. The image of immortality can connect with the experience of spiritual death and rebirth which may occur many times during one's earthly existence. Spiritual rebirth in this sense may be interpreted as a dying to profane or vulgar existence and a regenerated life on a more intense and meaningful plane, an experience that gives rise to profound and revitalizing hope. The Jewish religion has emphasized rebirth as something that happens to the whole people or nation. Christianity has focused more on individual spiritual attainment and salvation.

Imagery of rebirth is found in the Hindu and Buddhist as well as the Jewish and Christian religions. And whenever such imagery is present, the danger of its being literalized is always present, too. But central to all these traditions, and more compatible with our own psychoformative position, is the conception of transcending death through spiritual attainment that connects one with eternal principles.

Thus the idea of being "chosen by God," experiencing the grace of God, or in Eastern religions, removing the veil of ordinary existence—all these images speak symbolically of a changed experience of time and of death somehow losing its sting. Whether through prayer, worship, contemplation, or meditation, all religions have taught methods of reorienting oneself in relation to time and death. This reorientation is often spoken of as a spiritual rebirth that must be preceded by a death of the old self. This is expressed in the Christian tradition in the words "He who finds his life will lose it, and he who loses his life for my sake will find it," a paradoxical image suggesting both death and rebirth.

A fourth mode is the sense of immortality achieved through continuity with *nature*. "From dust you come and to dust you shall return" is an Old Testament injunction against pride, as well as an expression of confidence that the earth itself does not die. Whatever happens to man, the trees, mountains, seas, and rivers endure. Partly for this reason, we constantly go back to nature, however briefly, for spiritual refreshment and revitalization.

In traditional Japanese culture, nature has been seen as a divine embodiment of the gods of mountain, valley, rain, wind, field, and stream. The delicate beauty of Japanese gardens is an expression of this cultural legacy. In India, the gods are always pictured as residing amidst lush mountains and valleys—nature being the ideal spiritual home. Americans, too, have had an intense concern with the "great outdoors," a concern originally demonstrated by the importance of the great frontier—that ever expanding horizon of the earthly realm of man.

The image of nature as the great frontier still exists in our journeys to the moon and aspirations beyond. (These journeys and aspirations, being human, become corrupted by the competitive insistence of a single nation upon being the first there—in effect, upon claiming an immortalizing advantage for this priority.) An avid interest in outdoor sports of all kinds and a growing preoccupation with ecology witness the continuing importance of being in touch with a surviving natural habitat. The concern with ecology has arisen from the very real possibility of the destruction of the environment, and also from the continuing importance of nature for our imaginations. In this sense, the enduring rhythms of nature have a significance that is undiminished, and perhaps intensified, for those city-dwellers to whom they are no longer visible.

A fifth mode of immortality, which we call *experiential transcendence,* is a bit different from the others in that it depends solely on a psychological state. This state is the experience of illumination or rapture attained as time seems to disappear. The term transcendence—meaning "going beyond"—refers to the feeling of being beyond the limits and confines of ordinary daily life. Moments of transcendence have an ecstatic quality, and the word "ecstasy" means "to stand outside of"—to be outside of oneself. In this sense, moments of experiential transcendence are moments of being beyond prosaic life, and beyond death.

Experiential transcendence is similar to the spiritual reorientation which we spoke of as religious rebirth. But such psychological experience may also be found in music, dance, battle, athletics, mechanical flight, contemplation of the past, artistic or intellectual creation, sexual love, childbirth, comradeship, and the feeling of working together with others in common cause. This experience can occur in relation to any of the other four modes (biological, creative, theological, natural) and, in fact, may be essential in order to integrate any of them into one's life. However it occurs, experiential transcendence involves a sense of timelessness, of which Jung spoke. There does seem to be a universal psychic potential and even need for occasional suspension of ordinary awareness of time.

The state of experiential transcendence may be brought on with the aid of drugs, starvation, physical exhaustion, or lack of sleep. However induced, this state is felt as involving extraordinary psychological unity, intensity of sensual awareness, and unexpressible illumination and insight. After such an experience, life is not quite the same. In fact, it is the result of such experiences—the sense of "new life"—that is often valued more than the experiences themselves.

Transcendent experiences result in a reordering of the dominant symbols and images by which one lives. The result can be a new tone of vitality in living, a new sense of commitment to one's projects, or the abandoning of one's old projects and commitments in favor of a totally new style of life. The reordering can also lead to greater ethical integrity and more courageous moral actions. Experiences of this kind can be of greater or lesser intensity. But even such relatively less intense and more common occurrences as exertion on a tennis court or in a sprint, a moment of insight or quietude, or gentle sensual touching can involve an altered sense of time and a feeling of expanded life space.

Over the centuries, men have frequently used drugs in pursuit of these experiences. In recent years drugs have been increasingly used, often in combination with music, to achieve various kinds of "highs." Many people in describing such "trips" have emphasized the importance of the setting in which the drug is taken, the person with whom one shares the experience (the "guide"), and the expectations that one brings to the experience. All these refer to the symbolic context or set of images present in the mind prior to and during the use of the drug. This, in turn, suggests that drugs *by themselves* do not bring about spiritual reorientation. Large numbers of people are finding forms of spiritual discipline, such as meditation, which can offer similar experiences without recourse to drugs.

The "highs" which some people experience with drugs (or alcohol) are obtained by other people in different ways. William James long ago remarked that getting drunk was the poor man's substitute for what the rich get from going to the symphony. Whether that is precisely true or no, we might wonder what he would say now about the more modern combination of listening stoned to the Stones. In any case it is interesting that the use of marijuana has come to be termed getting "stoned"—almost in the way getting drunk is sometimes referred to as being "plastered." In each case the image is of becoming desensitized, even inanimate—but in a very special way that is thought of as highly pleasurable and beyond pain. Although alcohol is primarily a depressant and marijuana characteristically intensifies perception, both can result in either heightened sensitivity or the reverse, depending upon the setting and the expectations that one brings to their use.

Those who would connect the use of drugs with the experience of transcendence (as we are doing here) are nevertheless compelled to recognize the addiction and deterioration which can also result.

The deaths of Janis Joplin and Jimi Hendrix, for example, suggest the way in which drug use may involve the user in destructive experiences, even death trips.

When reordering and renewal give way to exclusive reliance upon the chemical influence of the drug, habituation and addiction can be said to occur. No longer having access to liberating images, the "old self" remains in a state of symbolic death. Use of the drug then becomes more desperate, and the breakdown of inner integrity becomes increasingly associated with the death imagery of separation, disintegration, and stasis. The anxiety associated with these impels the user to return even more desperately to the drug in a pathetic downward spiral. There are many people whose relationship to drugs is a mixture of these extremes, containing elements of symbolic reordering and rebirth as well as habituation and anxiety.

The quest for experiential transcendence is usually related not only to the search for the new, but also to the unfolding of that which is oldest and deepest in the self. Rebirth and new life are recurrent images in all religious traditions; the Christian spiritual message is, in fact, referred to as "good *news*." The experience of addiction, not only to drugs but to anything else as well, is a desperate search for novelty (always a new high) with continually less experience that is actually new. Thus, addiction comes to be the experience that nothing is new—a nullification of the life imagery of movement. It becomes instead a deathlike numbness from which recovery is difficult.

The process of therapy in psychiatry involves a symbolic reordering analogous to that which occurs in experiential transcendence. When therapy is successful, a patient feels a widening of the space in which he lives. It is as if the narrow images through which he has seen reality have been reorganized so that the past appears more coherent and the future more inviting. Death imagery is reconceived, and life imagery of connection, integrity, and movement becomes dominant.

In many societies experiential transcendence is encouraged through fiestas, festivals, holidays, and celebrations which help people to break free of the restraints of routine and to sing, dance, drink, laugh, and love in a spirit of excess. Such celebrations radically interrupt ordinary daily life and allow participants to forget time and responsibility. The occasions for these celebrations are often religious holy days which derive from society's myth of its own beginnings. The celebration is a kind of birthday in which the society's birth is commemorated and its people's lives renewed.

Experiential transcendence is thus a key to the sense of immortality in any mode. For what lies at the heart of experiential transcendence—reorientation of time—is necessary to the other modes as well if they are in fact to connect with a sense of the eternal. Experiential transcendence involves entry into what has been called "mythic time," in which the perception of death is minimized and the threat of extinction is no longer foreboding. One feels oneself alive in a "continuous present" in which ancient past and distant future are contained.

We spoke earlier of the innate death imagery of separation, disintegration, and stasis. The five modes of symbolic immortality provide avenues through which the death anxiety associated with these images can be mastered. By achieving significant relation to these modes, one's life assumes qualities of continuity and the life imagery of connection, movement, and integrity is affirmed. We can speak of the need to master death anxiety as basic to the human condition, and we can see the modes of symbolic immortality as providing paths for this mastery.

It is possible to think of human life at every moment as moving between two poles: imagery of total severance (death imagery) and imagery of continuity (symbolic immortality). Both are present in a kind of balance; neither is able totally to abolish the other. Death imagery makes the quest for symbolic immortality more urgent and provides a stimulus for creative effort of all kinds. Images of continuity and immortality make the certainty of death less threatening. Feeling moments of experiential transcendence or a strong sense of relation to one of the other modes of symbolic immortality enables one to affirm the continuity of life without denying death. Much of the time these matters are not part of conscious awareness, although they underlie and support the tone and quality of one's awareness. At crisis points and times of transition, however, they become very conscious issues.

Periods of historical dislocation are characterized by lack of confidence in a society's institutions. But institutions—family, church, government, work, schools—are themselves structures through which to facilitate the sharing of images of immortalizing connectedness. In times like our own when these institutions are in flux, the task for each individual of maintaining a sense of immortality becomes vastly more difficult.

Death anxiety becomes overwhelming when one has to confront it in isolation. Societies and social institutions—when people believe in them —are able to aid in mastering death anxiety by generating shared images of continuity beyond the life of each single person. The capacity to live with death is generated by available social forms as well as by forms made available by one's own life.

Suicide is therefore never a purely private matter. When a person takes his own life, not only does he demonstrate his own failure to master death anxiety; he reveals a social failure as well. The society has not managed to share with him its symbols of continuity. In committing suicide a person makes a once-and-for-all total effort to master death anxiety.

Paradoxically, suicide can be an attempt to assert symbolic integrity: It is a way of holding to certain principles, of actively defining one's life boundaries, and of affirming value. This is not to say that suicide does not result from despair. But to live with despair is one thing; to perform the final act of ending one's life is another. Suicide can be seen as a kind of false mastery: One commits suicide when one is unable to live with the knowledge of death or envision a viable connection beyond it.

That suicide cannot be understood solely as an act of valueless despair is shown by the traditional Japanese practice of hara-kiri. In this act of ritual suicide, dying with dignity overcomes the humiliation of defeat. In accordance with the samurai code, suicide is an honorable act through which one can maintain the purity and immortality of one's name and country and, in the act of dying, reassert immortalizing principles. Yukio Mishima, the great Japanese novelist, attempted to revive that tradition and to convey in his recent suicide the message that contemporary Japan is losing its national essence. Though many found his act of ritual suicide absurd, it had a profound impact on Japanese society.

What about other kinds of suicide? Certainly not everyone who commits suicide lives by so demanding a code as that of the samurai. Nevertheless, a person who voluntarily ends his life is asserting in a positive way—although through a negative act —that under certain conditions life is not endurable. The act of suicide thus presumes the presence of some standards as to what a livable life would be. Under extreme conditions, such as Nazi extermination camps, suicide could become an assertion of freedom (to take one's own life rather than to wait to be killed) and even an inspiration for rebellion. For this to happen, suicide must be associated with a vision of life renewal beyond the death-dominated moment.

Suicide can rarely be the source of such renewal. More characteristically, it is the ultimate failure to master that which can never be completely mastered: death itself. But destructive and self-destructive acts are less likely to be resorted to when one feels oneself to be animated by a sense of immortality.

4

Death and History

Man creates culture by changing natural conditions in order to maintain his spiritual self.
—OTTO RANK, from
"The Double as
Immortal Self"

What we call "history" is the record of the experiences of a people, nation, or culture. These collectivities are, of course, composed of individual people. So it would seem logical to suppose that if we understood the psychology of individual persons, then we would at the same time understand both human groups and human history. But the history of a society is more than the sum of the histories of the individuals that make up that society.

A psychologically based theory of history, therefore, would require explanatory concepts sensitive enough and yet sufficiently broad to connect private individual actions to the public and collective events we call history. The discipline of psychohistory (a blend of psychology and history) takes as its task the finding of such concepts.

Death imagery has been largely ignored both in individual psychology and in attempts to apply psychology to history. But we believe that the human problems of mastering death anxiety and achieving a sense of immortality are tasks that individuals cannot accomplish alone. These are issues

77

at the common boundary of the individual life project and the collective historical project.

When we speak of individual lives and collective history as "projects," we mean to emphasize two things: first, that there is a forward sense of vision and movement and, second, that something is being made, constructed. In his effort to move forward, man requires symbols of continuity and flow; these symbols take shape within the modes of immortality. *From the viewpoint of the individual* we can say that the life project is to achieve significant relation to one or more of these modes. *From the broader viewpoint of history* we can say that the collective cultural life project is to maintain the viability of the modes of immortality so that they will continue to provide avenues for individual personal fulfillment.

Cultures must evolve some way of dealing with death, but they do so with varying capacities for acknowledging the fact that man is mortal. Death can be radically denied, as in primitive religions which do not admit such a thing as natural death. But this kind of denial is tenuous. It creates an atmosphere of profound suspiciousness, for if death is not natural, then it must result from "unnatural" occurrences such as curses or spells.

Many cultures have buried their dead with tools and weapons in order for them to continue life in another sphere, or have practiced ancestor worship out of the conviction that the dead continued to exercise authority. Burying tools with the dead suggests both denial and acceptance of death. It supports the illusion that the dead will need tools (and thus not really be dead), and, at the same time, symbolizes the feeling that despite individual deaths, the culture's work and life will go on.

A theory which links death imagery with history must emphasize the struggle to live with the anxiety that death imagery arouses. Men and women can deal with this anxiety by relating themselves to the modes of symbolic immortality which are combined and expressed in constantly changing ways. The struggle is to maintain the meaningfulness of particular expressions of the sense of immortality, or to find new expressions, as historical conditions change. This makes it possible, in a more complex way, *to affirm life in the face of death.*

One way to understand human history is to see it as *the effort to achieve, maintain, or reaffirm a collective sense of immortality under constantly changing conditions.* For the modes of immortality to be meaningful, they must relate to the particular kinds of experience characteristic of a given historical period. The forms and expressions of human continuity which sufficed for ancient Greek culture or even nineteenth-century American culture will not do for us today. But this is not to say that the struggle itself is obsolete—only that new forms and expressions can and must evolve. The overall tendency of historical and religious thought has been away from literal biological immortality bestowed by impersonal cosmic forces or supernatural gods, and toward a more symbolized continuity of human culture that includes each individual life.

Cultural values give support to individuals in their efforts to master death anxiety by establishing notions of what it means to live a good and productive life. In order to be effective, these values must embrace one or more of the modes of immortality with enough intensity to affirm individual strivings toward connection, integrity, and movement at their deepest psychic levels.

Cultural ideals of what constitutes a worthwhile life change over time and at some critical points become unclear or caught in conflict with rival notions. In our own time in the United States, the dominant culture holds forth a model of ideal adulthood that emphasizes the importance of good education, holding a steady job, settling down, raising a family, and achieving measurable goals—all within existing social and technological arrangements. Simultaneously, a counterculture has developed as a collective critique of these standards, and, while characterized by continuous experiment, it contains its own identifiable values. The counterculture chooses to live communally rather than in small, isolated families, self-expression rather than conformity to "job requirements," and enjoyment and realization in the present rather than continual postponement of pleasure. Yet, even in its stress on the present, the counterculture seeks to connect with and create enduring principles.

Representative figures of the counterculture like Bob Dylan, Ram Dass, and Tom Hayden personify new ideals of a more rebellious, expressive, and playful adulthood. Both old and new models of adulthood, and the many combinations in between that characterize most of our lives, offer styles and world views sufficiently diverse to permit people to find their individual pathways.

We can speak of "group mastery" of death anxiety as involving the successful connection of shared institutionalized values with individual convictions and needs. The outer world of culture (institutions, beliefs, values) must connect powerfully with the perceptions and feelings of individuals about their own lives. *Psychohistorical dislocation* is characterized by the failure of cultural symbols to connect in significant ways with individual strivings. There is a gap between *outer* cultural life and *inner* psychological reality. The result is intensification of death anxiety and the need to deny the reality of death. The task of "getting one's head together" then involves finding a form for one's life that, in turn, fits within the framework of larger, more enduring social forms.

The emergence of the counterculture in the 1960's suggests what can happen in such a crisis. As old ideas, values, and symbols lose their power for many people, attempts are made to evolve new symbols and life-styles to replace or revitalize the old ones. Such a process is painful and slow, both because symbols that have the capacity to move large numbers of people are not invented easily and because old values are not expelled quickly even from the lives of people who chafe under them. But if the crisis of the old culture is profound, the demand for regeneration and renewal becomes urgent. The experience becomes one of feeling that the old must die both within and without if life is to remain possible. This kind of urgency lies behind revolutionary change of all kinds.

Great turning points in history can be understood as major modifications or recombinations of the modes of symbolic immortality. The transformation in human consciousness brought about (and the process is by no means complete) by the work of Charles Darwin in the mid-nineteenth century on evolution involved a shift in modes. While not denying that God had a hand in creation, Darwin emphasized that natural creation is a continuing process begun millions of years ago. His focus was on the natural rather than the divine aspects of the life process.

Darwin's work caused an intense public debate, and even now there are some who refuse to accept his ideas because they conflict with the literal teachings of the Bible. The passionate quality of this dispute reveals that real life and death issues (in symbolic form) are involved. This is comprehensible if we realize that the Darwinian revolution entailed a shift in modes from the theological to the biological and the natural. Thus, the debate concerned the ultimate issue of forms of human continuity and aroused the death anxiety that always lurks behind struggles over modes of immortality.

The Communist revolution in China over the last few decades has resulted in the creation of a new society. These changes are expressed in the leadership of Mao Tse-tung and epitomized by his famous red book of writings. But China's twentieth-century social transformation can be seen as a profound alteration of the modes of immortality previously dominant in China. The emphasis has shifted from biological immortality (the importance of an individual's family and ancestors emphasized in Confucian ethics) to the entire Chinese people as a revolutionary community. The idea of creative works has been extended and is now based on contribution to the revolution rather than on individual accomplishment. The mode of experiential transcendence has been very much present in ecstatic moments of revolutionary activity, as during the Cultural Revolution of the late 1960's.

Shifts in these modes require decades or centuries to take hold, but they are often represented by a single person (like Darwin or Mao) or a single event (like the dropping of the atomic bomb on Hiroshima). Spiritual heroes like Buddha, Moses, and Christ are associated with new or renewed theological modes and represent for their followers sacred models of how to live in a way that enables them to master death. But man's spiritual desperation is sometimes such that he sees as heroes and "death conquerors" violent leaders like Hitler whose aberrant quest for immortality requires an endless flow of corpses.

Because human images of continuity can assume a limitless number of forms, the modes of immortality can be varied in an unending series as diverse as the dreams and lives of individual people. Human inventiveness in the pursuit of immortality testifies to the persistent urgency of avoiding death anxiety.

The modes of immortality are essentially categories of human experience. They are, as we have said, categories that are at once both personal and more than personal. For this reason, they provide a link between the lives of individuals and the historical process. We can speak of psychohistorical dislocation as involving *impaired symbolic immortality*—meaning that the threat is felt both at the personal and at the cultural level. The combination in the last thirty years of accelerating historical change and nuclear age danger has produced such a crisis. Man's relationship to each of the modes has been fundamentally altered. (This process is examined in detail in Chapter 5.) Because man's image of himself and his world is fragmented, there is an ample opportunity for rebuilding—if one knows where to begin. The absence of clear social forms often gives us the contradictory sense that everything and nothing is possible.

The loss of a sense of immortality can lead to desperate measures in the attempt to master death anxiety. One such measure is "ideological totalism," in which a system of ideas is held with absolute conviction, regardless of how well or badly these ideas fit the complexity of reality. Totalism is an all-or-none proposition in which some political, religious, or philosophical creed is raised to the level of an all-encompassing claim to truth.

It is important to see the dangers inherent in a totalistic orientation and to distinguish this clearly from more ordinary forms of belief. In subscribing to a totalistic view of the world, one avoids the discomfort of having to check one's beliefs against one's perceptions ("Does what I believe fit with reality?") and has instead the comfort of always knowing in advance where one stands. The belief is total—it answers all questions. Beliefs and values no longer serve as *guides* for action; in their absolute authority they both describe reality and prescribe right action.

The impulse to evolve a totalistic conception of reality bears some resemblance to the more usual human impulse to find a familiar realm or space. The familiar space is that which is known and trusted and in which one can relax. People customarily distinguish between other people whom they do not know (strangers) and those who are familiar (family, neighbors, friends). But ordinarily some process of familiarization is possible, whereby those who are strangers can become known, trusted, and included in the category of neighbors and friends as the circle of known space widens.

A totalistic view allows for no such process or allows it only if the strangers are exactly like oneself. The space which one inhabits ("space" here including ideas one holds and people one accepts, as well as geographical area) becomes *sacred*. Those outside the sacred space are conceived as ghosts, demons, foreigners, or, simply, the enemy. And the enemy is he who must be destroyed—killed—if one's own group is to remain alive.

In creating an absolute picture of the world, totalism thus makes at the same time absolute distinctions between in-groups and out-groups. We mentioned a similar tendency for exclusion of others in our discussion of adolescent cliques. The motivation in each case is basically the same: to bolster one's own confidence in the face of death anxiety by demonstrating the power to oppress others. This, we believe, is the driving force behind all forms of prejudice. We use the word "victimization" rather than prejudice to emphasize that the process is not merely one of the individual idiosyncratic attitudes. The capacity to create victims draws upon individual psychological tendencies but emerges in relation to a psychohistorical process that begins with dislocation and culminates in violence. And we would stress that this process is primarily an expression of cultural symbolization rather than of instinctual drives toward death or aggression.

Historical examples of this process are, unfortunately, plentiful. The Spanish Inquisition in the fifteenth century ruthlessly exterminated those who were suspected of deviating from official religious doctrine. And in our own century, the German persecution of Jews in World War II death camps was rationalized as being necessary to preserve racial and cultural purity. In these cases, as always in the victimizing process, the victimized group was viewed as less than human, as tainted with death. Because they have been tainted with death, killing them is not really killing.

This whole totalizing and victimizing process can be seen as a kind of counterfeit immortality. It achieves for one's own group a sense of being elevated above the threshold of death only by reducing the status of another group: One man's immortality is bought at the cost of another's. One might be tempted to call this the "cheap" route to immortality were it not so extraordinarily costly to human life. Perhaps more aptly we can describe victimization as *the psychologically cowardly path to immortality*.

Over the course of history, victimization has been motivated by the assumption that immortality is the prerogative of a dominant caste, class, race, religion, and, more recently, technological power. In ancient Egypt, only the Pharaoh and his nobles were awarded this prerogative. In the Calvinist religion, only those chosen by the grace of God would re-

Death and History

ceive salvation, with economic success sometimes viewed as evidence of having been so chosen. In both cases, the low status of ordinary people was interpreted as an indication that they were not favored by divine forces in this world or the next, and, therefore, not entitled to salvation.

The caste system in India also reflects a correlation between social position and the right to immortality, though today it is considerably weaker than in ages past and, in fact, by law no longer exists. The law of karma in Hindu theology makes one's condition in this incarnation dependent upon one's behavior in a prior life. A completely faultless life could earn one liberation from the necessity of having to be born again and thereby free one's soul forever.

In both India and Japan, outcast groups have been thought of as defiled and polluted. These people have been relegated to the death-tainted professions: the handling of dead bodies for burial and cremation, slaughtering and butchering of animals, leather work, and the handling of human excrement. The Japanese have even tended to ignore these persons completely, to the extent of not including them in the census figures of total population. The Hindus in India have at times gone even farther. In many places, lower-caste Indians could not walk the same streets as those born into higher castes; if they did walk these streets they had to carry a broom to brush away their footprints. They could not even spit on the ground; the ground was reserved for the spittle of upper castes only. So the lower-caste people wore a small container on their necks into which they could spit. Before entering a street, these lower-caste persons were required to shout a warning so that holier persons could escape their contaminating shadows.

Lest such extreme examples seem exotic and remote, it is well to remember that only one hundred years have passed since the American Civil War, prior to which black slaves were bought and sold like cattle—a practice that was also rationalized with religious doctrine. Subsequent treatment of blacks in America, while not generally so extreme, has continued to express patterns of victimization.

For a black in America, skin color has been the main criterion around which discrimination has occurred. In many parts of the world, blackness has been associated with impurity and death, and whiteness with purity and immortality. Such examples as black magic, the black plague, and the use of black for funerals and mourning suggest a widespread psychological tendency to associate the color black with death. In many countries, dark-skinned peoples themselves have developed prejudicial judgments based on darkness of skin. In some places (like America), this has been the result of capitulating to the dominant racist values of the white society. But it has occurred independently of white influence as well. Of importance here is the association of darkness with the color of feces (dead matter) and with the darkness of night (the frightening aspects of night being attributed to dark people).

The reasons for victimization of dark-skinned people are complex and not entirely clear. What remains striking throughout history, however, is the human tendency to create victims of one kind or another. This tendency can be associated with economic distinctions, caste, class, religion, or race, but is not entirely explained by any of these. Without fail, the victimizing group holds an image of the victims as in some way not fully human. But at the same time there is a tendency, never fully acknowledged, to see the victims as having some extraordinary powers, often great sexual prowess. The mythology in this country surrounding the strength and sexual capacities of black people is an illustration of this tendency.

How can one account for this contradictory image of the victims as at once less and more than human? The explanation may lie in the motivation for seeing other people as less than human in the first place: the need to assert one's own immortality by denying it to others. It may be that the victimizing group is never fully convinced that the victims are not really human, less entitled than they themselves to full claims on immortality. That is, the victimizers may not fully believe their own illusions. One can imagine an American slaveholder harboring deep doubts about whether his slaves are really less human than he.

The old saying "There but for the grace of God go I" reveals the human capacity for putting oneself in the shoes of victims. The recognition of oneself in an unfavored person (a slave; a victim of bomb, disease, or flood) is painful and is generally avoided. But it may be precisely this hidden recognition that perhaps *the victims really are human* that leads to a contrasting mythology that *the victims are more than human*. Moreover, once rendered nonhuman, the victims take on an exotic forbidden quality. This makes it possible to see victims as bizarre and superhuman. In the process of pursuing ideological totalism, victimizers often experience a separation of sexuality from affection and even from sensuality. The victimizer's sexuality becomes the desire for complete conquest and assertion of power; the victims are viewed as alluring but inhuman sexual monsters.

Psychologists use the word "ambivalence" to describe the tendency to have contradictory feelings about a person, object, experience, or relationship. Seeing victims as simultaneously less than human and superhuman thus reveals a profound ambivalence. This tendency is even clearer with respect to groups that we may term "elite victims." These are people who are seen as posing a threat to the victimizer's identity—and are for this reason made victims—but who are so bound up with the victimizer's cultural heritage that they have to be viewed with respect.

Within Western culture, Jews have had the status of elite victims. The Jewish and Christian traditions have held forth rival, though closely related, claims to immortality. The Jewish capacity to survive as a people, even in dispersion, and to survive with impressive cultural achievements, has aroused both respect and resentment. Jews have been heroic contributors to Western culture, and the Jewish tradition has been a vital part of Christian identity. Yet, the survival of the Jews has also been a continuing affront to Christian claims of universality. The Jewish refusal to accept Christ has been a deep irritant to certain Christian believers who from the time of Saint Paul have had their own inner doubts about the revelation.

This Christian need to create Jewish victims derives in part from the existence of these threatening rival claims to an immortalizing vision. But it may derive as well from resentment at the lack of realization of Jewish hopes themselves. The aspirations of Jewish culture—toward fidelity to the law and fidelity to one supreme God—have exerted great force on the imagination of the Western world. In making harsh and unrealized demands upon Western culture, and in offering a competing immortalizing vision, the Jews became both respected and hated.

The occupational roles of many Jews in Western Europe and America have been related to handling money—rather than handling feces or dead bodies, as with those who are more clearly victims. There is much evidence for unconscious association of money with feces and death. Not being permitted to own land, Jews were relegated to handling and lending money.

Money is both immortal and death-linked, and the handling of money is parallel to the handling of feces and dead bodies. Money is viewed more ambivalently: Money is a source of power, provides the means for a "good living," and enables one to leave something for descendants. But to say that "The love of money is the root of all evil," or "You can't take it with you" reflects an association of money with evil and even with death: "It is easier for a camel to get through the eye of a needle than for a rich man to enter heaven." Money is viewed with an ambivalence not unlike the attitudes that have prevailed toward Jews themselves as elite victims.

Jews, having established themselves in merchant

professions, have done extremely well in them; many have, in fact, prospered and become wealthy. As in Germany in the 1930's, many non-Jews perceived that the Jews were, so to speak, out-immortalizing them, a situation that prompted the non-Jews to rationalize their role as victimizers and the Jews as victims. This rationalization, in turn, generated more extreme forms of derogation and persecution.

Man's tendency to create victims, however ambivalent, leads only too directly to violence and butchery. Perceiving others as less than human renders the act of killing less than murder and, in fact, encourages killing in order to promote untainted "life." Extreme forms of physical torture and the killing of slaves were common in America's southern states. It has been argued that the slave system operated by the Spanish and Portuguese in South America was more human, less brutal, than that in the United States. A possible explanation is that in South America black slaves served chiefly as labor, while in the United States slaves were used both as sources of labor and as psychic victims. For the Spanish and Portuguese in South America, the Jews and Muslims (religious infidels) occupied the role of psychic victims—and were treated with extreme brutality—so that new ones were not needed.

We might conclude from this observation that men are capable of the most extreme destruction when they feel that their own life or the collective life of their people is threatened. Threats to man's symbols—his cultural representations of his own death-defying power—can quickly evoke death anxiety and provoke murder. In the South, the white woman, the southern belle, became the symbol of all that was pure and transcendent about southern life. The slightest suggestion of sexual contact between a white woman and a black slave (and one must always keep in mind that a taboo of this kind is always associated with special attraction) resulted immediately in harsh whippings or death for the slave. The white woman as ultimate symbol was defended with ultimate terror.

When political debate becomes the arena for the competition of rival immortalizing visions, the atmosphere is at once charged with extreme tension. Words no longer have just their literal meanings; they express as well philosophies held with religious passion. Friends become associates of God; enemies are seen as accomplices of the devil. The emotionally charged climate surrounding the discussion of Communism has had this quality. The threat posed by Communism is seen by the American political Right as something much more vast than simply that of political enemy. Communists are suspected of infiltrating and thereby polluting the American spirit itself. The American way of life, on the other hand, is defended as the very symbol of God's vision of life on earth.

Particular contempt is reserved by true believers for those who are seen as potential allies but who refuse to lend support to (or who abandon) a particular cause or belief. For this reason, Jews have historically been a thorn in the side of Christian believers. Within Communist China, deviant ideas about the right course for China have been attacked with intense fervor. In the United States, both in the McCarthyite anti-Communist witch hunts of the

1950's and the Nixon Administration's list of Presidential enemies, there was a shift from the concept of a political opponent to that of the "subversive" and the "enemy" who could then be victimized.

If psychohistorical dislocation leads to totalism, and then to victimization and violence, what can we say of the victim's response to his situation? There are several alternatives that have been followed, none of them very satisfactory. One course is for the victim to try to become like the victimizer, so as to claim for himself something of the state of immortality the victimizer appears to possess. Thus, inmates in Nazi concentration camps have tried to imitate their guards, Jews in ordinary society have tried to "act like gentiles," Negroes to "pass" for white. The victim may go even farther in his imitation and attempt to victimize his fellows in order to acquire even more of the victimizer's power.

Or the victim may attempt to reverse the immortalizing standards: the black refusing to be a "nigger," the National Liberation Front soldier in Vietnam refusing to be a "gook." In the struggle for dignity and for an identity outside of being a victim, the blacks have developed and embraced the idea that black is beautiful. In this process, blacks may require a turning inward and a certain amount of exclusiveness to develop pride, which may then make possible genuine mutuality or coexistence as equals with whites. But it could also lead them to their own forms of victimization, simply reversing the roles.

The more difficult path is a long and painful struggle on the part of victims for authentic identity not solely dependent upon the previous experience

of having been victimized. They must develop and
generate their own social energy rather than rely on
the help of victimizers. Yet, some form of help is
often required, and this too the victims know. They
want and deserve help but are wary of accepting it,
lest they be reminded of their previous status as
helpless victims. The needed help is seen as a kind
of "counterfeit nurturance," and there is the urge to
accept it as well as to throw it back in the faces
of the donors. Much of the black struggle in America for autonomy and dignity has involved these excruciating tensions.

Frantz Fanon, a gifted West Indian psychiatrist
and revolutionary, has described and interpreted the
struggles of long-colonialized peoples to achieve autonomy. He stresses the psychological dimension of
colonization and decolonization and the necessity
for colonized "natives" to reclaim not only their
countries, but also their dignity and pride. For these
oppressed peoples, Fanon writes, feeling powerful
must originate in feeling able to kill the old oppres-
sors, and that power must be demonstrated in actual
killing.

There is profound psychological truth in Fanon's
position, especially in his stress on former victims'
need to discover their own autonomy and power in
order to break out of the victimizing process. Yet
if Fanon's message is taken literally and vengefully,
it can lead to the reinstitution of victimization, this
time in the name of liberation.

If there is a way out of this seemingly hopeless
impasse, it must involve a fresh act of rebirth, an
act of imagination that regenerates and renews the
sources of immortality. Such leaps of imagination are

rare but possible. Gandhi led the Indians to assert themselves against the British *precisely by refusing violence*. He thus envisioned a biosocial mode of immortality broad enough for both British and Indians. This spiritual and immortalizing victory he substituted for the bloody battle that otherwise seemed inevitable. Young Americans who resisted the Vietnam war, as well as those who fought in it and then opposed it, also sought to relate themselves to this mode.

5

The Nuclear Age

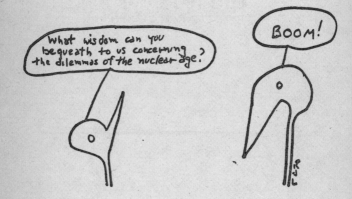

The seventeenth century was the century of mathematics, the eighteenth that of the physical sciences, and the nineteenth that of biology. Our twentieth century is the century of fear.

—ALBERT CAMUS, from
Neither Victims Nor Executioners

The sun can't hold a candle to it.
•
Now we're all sons of bitches.

—Two reactions of nuclear scientists to the first atomic bomb test

---

Early in the morning of August 6, 1945, the United States dropped on the Japanese city of Horoshima the first atomic bomb ever used on a human population. The destruction and chaos wrought by that bomb were so immense that it has never been possible to make a precise count of the number of people killed. Most estimates are in the range of 100,000 to 200,000 people. Even for the hundreds of thousands who experienced the bombing but remained alive, the vision and taint of nuclear holocaust left lifelong scars.

The bomb was unexpected; it came as people

went about their morning chores of making and eating breakfast and preparing to go to work. Suddenly a blinding flash cut across the sky. There were a few seconds of dead silence and then a huge explosion. Enormous clouds formed and then rose upward in a gigantic dark column. The clouds leveled off and the whole formation resembled an enormous black mushroom.

Those who have seen atomic explosions speak of their awesome and frightening beauty. On that Japanese summer morning, the beauty was immediately eclipsed by the experience of an overwhelming encounter with death. Normal existence had suddenly been massively invaded by an eerie and unknown force. An area of total destruction was created extending for two miles in all directions, and 60,000 buildings within the city limits were demolished.

The reaction of the survivors was at first a sense of being totally immersed in death. Houses and buildings leveled, the sight of dead bodies, the cries and moans of the severely injured, and the smell of burning flesh all combined to leave a permanent death imprint of staggering power.

Among the survivors there quickly developed a profound kind of guilt. This guilt was related both to having remained alive while others (including loved ones and neighbors) died and to the inability to offer help to those who needed it. All of this became focused in a question that remained at the center of a lifelong struggle for the survivors: "Why did I remain alive when he, she, they died?" And this question itself sometimes became transformed into the haunting suspicion that one's own life had been purchased at the cost of the others who died: "Some had to die; because they died I could live." This suspicion led to a feeling among survivors that they did not deserve to be alive and that one could justly remain alive only by coming in some way to resemble the dead.

The Japanese survivors became psychologically numb, their sensitivities blunted by guilt and by an inability to resume meaningful activity amid the chaos. The boundary separating life from death no longer seemed distinct. By becoming numb, the survivors blocked their awareness of the pain and suffering and effected a kind of compromise between life and death.

The survivors' lives were made even more difficult by a susceptibility to various forms of disease and weakness to which their exposure to atomic radiation made them vulnerable. Many of those exposed have had to struggle to live with maimed bodies; all have had to live with the incredible end-of-the-world image of nuclear holocaust.

For us, now, the image of Hiroshima symbolizes the possibility that what has happened once can happen again. By today's standards, that first atomic bomb was a very small one. The difficulty of imagining the human suffering that followed in the wake of its use is multiplied many times over in trying to contemplate what a world war with atomic weapons would be like now.

The atomic bomb was the product of an extraordinary research program carried out during World War II. In the beginning there had been little confidence that an atomic bomb could actually be made. But the suspicion that German scientists were attempting to put such a weapon into the hands of Hitler led the United States to undertake an all-out effort.

In 1939, a letter to President Roosevelt was drafted by Albert Einstein encouraging full support for a scientific program that would lead to the development of the atomic bomb. Research installations were established at a number of places throughout the country, and work went ahead with unprecedented commitment. By July, 1945, the first atomic bomb was ready for testing in the New Mexico desert. So intense was the effort to create the bomb and so anxious were the scientists about whether it would work that few physicists at Los Alamos were inclined to raise moral questions about the weapon they made.

The bomb worked. Suddenly, it became possible for one plane to deliver a single bomb the explosive power of which previously would have required two thousand bombs. All who watched were awestruck by what they saw; the experience had a religious quality. Men had released through the bomb a source of power literally beyond imagining. It seemed that the use of this powerful device could bring the war to a rapid conclusion and could in peacetime yield untold energy, and would thus transform the nature of both war and peace.

All these things were possible. But what were immediate and overwhelming were the sheer majesty and power of the bomb itself. J. Robert Oppenheimer, director of the research project that produced the bomb, later remembered his thoughts at the time of the explosion:

> At that moment . . . there flashed into my mind a passage from the Bhagavad-Gita, the sacred book of the Hindus: "I am become Death, the Shatterer of Worlds!"

Another observer at the time used such phrases as "mighty thunder" and "great silence" to describe his response, and went on to speak in clearly religious language:

> On that moment hung eternity. Time stood still. Space contracted to a pinpoint. It was as though the earth had opened and the skies had split. One felt as though he had been privileged to witness the Birth of the World.

Others had more cynical responses: "Now we're all sons of bitches," and, more simply, "What a thing we've made." Still others spoke of "the dreadful," "the terrible," "the dire," and "the awful."

"This is the greatest thing in history!" was President Truman's response upon hearing of the bomb's successful use in Hiroshima, which seemed to portend a rapid end to the war. And a newspaper report at the time described the force as "weird, incredible, and somehow disturbing."

If we understand the experience of religious conversion as involving a changed image of the cosmos and man's place within it, then certainly the responses of those early witnesses to atomic power would quality as religious. There was a sense of a "new beginning," of making contact with the infinite and the feeling that life would never be the same again. The bomb took on qualities of a deity, a god whose strange and superhuman power would change the course of human history.

After it became clear that this atomic god was real, the scientists who had unleashed it began to diverge in their responses to the new power. As in any situation, most went on with their professional "business as usual." Some assumed a sense of mission in committing themselves to controlling the use of this threatening force. Others identified themselves with the force, became converts to the religion of nuclearism, and dedicated themselves to propagating the new faith.

Nuclearism is a peculiar, twentieth-century disease of power. We would do well to specify it, trace its roots, and see its connection with other forms of religious and immortalizing expression. Nuclearism is a form of totalism. It yields a grandiose vision of man's power at a historical time when man's precarious sense of his own immortality makes him particularly vulnerable to such aberrations.

Man has always attached deep emotion to his tools. As extensions of his own body and capacities, they have provided him with an image of himself. The centrality of technology to twentieth-century culture has increased this tendency to define life in terms of the tools and techniques that have so deeply transformed the world. In this sense, nuclearism is a manifestation of two underlying contemporary inclinations: to deify tools and to seize whatever symbols are available in the desperate search for a sense of significance.

The career and personal struggles of J. Robert Oppenheimer reveal the tensions that have existed in relation to nuclear weapons. Oppenheimer directed the vast and complex research effort at Los Alamos. He and those with whom he worked were convinced that if the bomb could be developed quickly, its availability would hasten the end of the war and could even rid the world of war permanently. Certain nuclear scientists in Chicago who had completed their contribution to the bomb research project tried to raise moral questions about the bomb's use. Oppenheimer, however, remained committed and resisted such reflection. He did not agree that the bomb should merely be "demonstrated" to frighten the enemy into submission rather than be actually used on a human population.

It was not until 1949, when the vastly more powerful hydrogen bomb was nearly completed, that Oppenheimer began to re-examine his convictions. He continued to work on weapons research, and even came to favor the development of small "tactical" hydrogen bombs. But he became concerned that the idea of a "super" H-bomb seemed "to have caught the imagination, both of the Congressional and military people, as the answer to the problem posed by the Russians' advance." With his characteristic brilliance, Oppenheimer then began to expose the dangers involved in letting the bomb dominate all thinking on international relations.

Oppenheimer had been a national hero during and just after the war, when he was widely credited with the success of the atomic bomb research project. But when he began to raise questions about nuclearism and underwent what we might call "nuclear backsliding," he was forced to submit to extreme public humiliation in the form of a long government investigation of his "Americansim" and was eventually denied a security clearance. His earlier strong advocacy of the bomb and his national standing made his subsequent doubts all the more dangerous to those who remained proponents of nuclearism.

Edward Teller, another physicist important in early bomb research, who later became known as "the father of the hydrogen bomb," is representative of the opposite sequence. In 1945, Teller opposed the use of the atomic bomb without warning. After the war, he vehemently objected to the moral reservations expressed by other scientists toward the idea of making nuclear weapons. Teller advocated maintaining an "adventurous spirit" in fully exploring the possibilities of atomic weapons —which now meant "his" H-bomb—and he believed that "we would be unfaithful to the tradition of Western civilization if we shied away from exploring what man can accomplish." This combination of ethical blindness and extreme technicism, not just in Teller but in many others as well, inspired the subtitle of the film *Dr. Strangelove; or, How I Learned to Stop Worrying and Love the Bomb*.

No one could argue that the power of the atomic bomb is not impressive, or that it does not readily engender a sense of awe both for nature's power and man's capacity for technological mastery. But the danger of the nuclearist position is that the bomb's power and its limitations are never clearly examined. The terms that were used by the scientists in referring to the bomb—terms such as "the gadget," "the thing," "the device," or simply "It"—served to blunt a continuing awareness of the bomb's deadly purpose. The bomb became enmeshed in Utopian hopes for total salvation that seemed otherwise unattainable. Man's own place in the scheme of things was devalued and made subordinate to the demands of the weapon.

The early discussion of bomb shelters and diplomacy in the postwar period are examples of the perversions of logic to which the bomb led. It became clear that the United States could not fully defend itself from nuclear attack in case of another major war. An anxious debate ensued in which the chief issue was whether there would be any survivors of a major nuclear conflagration—shelters or no shelters. Also involved was the question of whether, considering the world into which they would emerge, the survivors would envy the dead. Teller argued that there *would* be survivors and that democratic ideals would survive with them. He insisted that "realistic thinking" demanded facing up to the possible consequences of the use of atomic weapons.

Given the experience of those who actually did survive the atomic bomb in Hiroshima, the question about survivors in this debate was never properly posed. The important question is not "Would there be survivors?" or "Would the survivors envy the dead?" but rather "Would the survivors themselves feel *as if* dead?"

Nuclearist thinking pervaded the field of diplomacy. There was a feeling that "the big atomic stick" (as Edward Teller called it) could solve the political problems of the world. There is no doubt that the presence of nuclear weapons did exercise a deterrent effect in international relations immediately following World War II. But a weapon too awesome and frightening to be used could not be a permanently effective deterrent. Statesmen began to realize that an arsenal consisting only of nuclear weapons would make the punishment for international violations more destructive than the crime. As one writer put it, a policeman armed only with an atomic bomb could not even prevent a housebreaking unless he were willing to sacrifice the entire city in doing so. It is even possible that the restraint on all-out war created by nuclear weapons made smaller, more prolonged conflicts like Vietnam more likely.

Nuclearism involves a failure of the imagination —a failure to conceive in human terms the meaning of the weapons—and, as a means of salvation, the embrace of that which most threatens human survival. Nuclearism provides an apocalyptic alternative to the already impaired modes of symbolic immortality while itself further undermining the viability of these modes. Nuclearism propels us toward use of the weapons and, equally dangerous, undermines man's capacity to confront the problems they raise.

Each of the modes of symbolic immortality has been affected by the dislocations of the nuclear era. Even without the actual deployment of these weapons, their very existence poses a profound threat to our perceptions of living and dying. The possibility that the human species can annihilate itself with its own tools fundamentally alters the relationship of human imagination to each mode of symbolic continuity.

The biological (and biosocial) mode is perhaps most obviously affected. The assumption of "living on" in one's descendents is made precarious. The aspiration of living on in one's nation is also undermined, for no longer do national boundaries offer the protection and security they once did. National security becomes identical with international security, which is dependent upon the partial relinquishment by each nation of its own exclusive claim on the allegiance of its citizens.

Because ultimate issues of life and death have become more urgent and more problematic, the theological mode has also become problematic. A rational-scientific age had already made commitments of religious faith and the meaning of God difficult issues for many people. Theological imagery of transcending death becomes a dubious promise if the assurance of some form of earthly survival is not also given. If there are none (or few) left among the biologically living, then the image of spiritual survival loses much of its symbolic and comforting power. It is precisely these threats to the belief in salvation that may account for the burgeoning of fundamentalist groups and the insistence of these groups upon the most narrow and literal—one might say desperate—forms of Biblical faith.

In Japan after the explosion of the atomic bomb, neither Eastern nor Western religious imagery seemed capable of providing an acceptable explanation or formulation of the meaning of the disaster. The bomb experience seems to have wounded that deep layer of human confidence and trust to which religious symbolism appeals. No conventional religious expression was adequate to re-establish a sense of trust and continuity.

Partly as a response to this impasse, religious language has come to emphasize the sacred quality of man's earthly commitments and the religious importance of responsible political action. At the same time, there has been a revival of fundamentalist and occult religion—a manifestation of the increased plausibility of apocalyptic visions. Who can now say that an image of the end of the world is merely a religious pipe dream meant to frighten people into submission?

Theological imagery has developed in two contrasting directions. There has been a movement toward naturalism, in which religious imagery is more humanistic and closer to observable process. But there has also been a rise of visionary and doomprophesying religious forms, in which salvation is made conditional upon total repentance. In either case, man's new demonic technological capcity (if not demonic human psychological potential) always threatens to overwhelm and render futile the attempt to immortalize man's spiritual attainments.

Immortality through the creative mode depends upon the conviction that one's works will endure. But what lasts anymore? The existence of nuclear weapons, together with the breakdown of the many forms of collective symbolization and ritual we have discussed, raises doubts about the permanence of any contributions to human culture. The fear is that nothing will last and that, therefore, nothing matters.

This concern about the viability of particular social forms and even about historical continuity itself creates an undercurrent of anxiety and mistrust that is generally not directly felt. But this concern is expressed in the increased need of young people to have a sense of the immediate human impact of their work and has resulted in heightened interest in careers involving teaching, legal practice, social work, and medicine. With regard to scientific work, as more questions are raised about the ethics of various scientific projects, the individual scientist is less able to undertake research without consideration of the lethal or life-enhancing potentials of the new knowledge he may unearth.

These questions and threats lead to a greater reliance upon the fourth mode—that of nature—for an image of permanence. But we now know that nature is all too susceptible to both our weapons and our pollution. Joan Baez's mournful tones in the song "What Have They Done to the Rain?" and Bob Dylan's desperate anger in "A Hard Rain's A-gonna Fall" both suggest a vision, shared by all of us in some degree, of ultimate nuclear violation of our planet.

In the face of this vision, explorations of outer space take on a special symbolic urgency. In these explorations we seek to extend our natural environment almost to infinity. But it would be the most wishful kind of illusion to see in these explorations, or in speculation about life on other planets, a solution to the problems of human continuity on our own endangered planet.

The impairment of these four modes of symbolic immortality has led to a greater reliance on the mode

111

of experiential transcendence. This mode is closely related to immediate sensation. It is therefore less vulnerable to being impoverished by misgivings about historical durability, on which the other modes are more dependent. To resort to pleasure-seeking or mystical experience is common in historically dislocated times. In our own time, we have witnessed great preoccupation with intensified forms of experience through drugs, sex, music, meditation, dance, nature, and even politics.

Beyond enabling one to live more fully in the present, the experiential mode lends itself to something more—to engaging death anxiety directly by experimenting with risk. Almost as artists become a community's conscience by exploring the extremities of the community's unfaced danger, the active pursuit of experiential transcendence plays with fears of death by inviting them, even encouraging them.

In this respect, there may be a strange parallel between nuclearism and the intense forms of experience that many people are now seeking. The most perverse response to the existence of a doomsday machine would be to love the bomb itself joyously: the nightmare of oblivion experienced as ecstasy. This is the malignant phenomenon that the film *Dr. Strangelove* carries even farther and portrays in a powerfully bizarre image: a cowboy euphorically riding an atomic bomb as it soars from the plane toward glorious explosion.

Fanciful as this image appears, it has an eerie psychological plausibility. Expressed boldly, there may be a need to destroy one's world for purposes of imagined rebirth, a need which lends itself either to suicidal obliteration or to transformation and regeneration. This need not only takes advantage of every variety of individual and social aggression, but fits as well with the psychological principle of touching death, either imaginatively or literally, as a precondition of new life. Thus, nuclear weapons can achieve vivid symbolic representation in our minds precisely because of their promise of devastation.

The ultimate threat posed by nuclear weapons is not only death but meaninglessness: an unknown death by an unimaginable weapon. War with such weapons is no longer heroic; death from such weapons is without valor. Meaninglessness has become almost a stereotyped characterization of twentieth-century life, a central theme in modern art, theater, and politics. The roots of this meaninglessness are many. But crucial, we believe, is the anxiety deriving from the sense that all forms of human associations are perhaps pointless because subject to sudden irrational ends. Cultural life thus becomes still more formless. No one form, no single meaning or style, appears to have any ultimate claim. The psychological implications of this formlessness are not fully clear; while there seem to be more life choices available, fewer are inwardly compelling.

Such broad historical themes as these can influence even the most fundamental of human relationships—the nurturing bond between mother and child. No mother can fully escape the general threat to the continuity and significance of life, or the resulting death anxiety. Nor can she avoid transmitting these doubts to her offspring. Erik Erikson has emphasized the importance for the child of gaining a sense of "basic trust" early in life. Lack of such a firm sense of basic trust can undermine one's self-confidence for life and can prevent an individual from fulfilling his creative potential. Such childhood deficiencies may result from a lack of parental trust, from misgivings in the parents about the meaning and significance of their own lives.

Fundamental attitudes like these are communicated to children in subtle ways from their earliest days on. The importance of symbolic impairments in parents, such as a lost sense of immortality, in producing individual psychological difficulties in children has not been much examined. But it is in such ways as this that the psychohistorical themes that characterize an era—like unfaced death anxiety in our time—become enmeshed in the psychological lives of individuals from one generation to another.

We began this chapter by describing some of the psychological struggles of those who survived the atomic bomb in Hiroshima. Those struggles involved guilt, numbing, and a continuing effort to give form and meaning to radically disrupted lives. Perhaps we can achieve little more than a glimmer of the excruciating tensions such extraordinarily painful lives have involved. But in another sense we are all survivors of this century's holocausts.

In cultivating and making clear to ourselves our own status as survivors, we become more fully part of the century in which we live. In doing so we open ourselves to the experience of pain and to the imagery and anxiety of death. We glimpse at such moments the necessity for personal and social transformation in the interest of continued survival and new meaning. The urgency of the tasks of reconstruction are then pressed upon us—though the forms our efforts must take are never fully clear.

6

Death and Rebirth:
The Survivor as Creator

In the worst night of my will,
I dared to question all

Caught in the dying light
I thought myself reborn.
> —THEODORE ROETHKE, from the
> poem "The Dying Man"

i thank You God for most this amazing
day:for the leaping greenly spirits of trees
and a blue true dream of sky, and for
    everything
which is natural which is infinite which is yes

(i who have died am alive again today,
and this is the sun's birthday; this is the birth
day of life and love and wings: and of the gay
great happening illimitably earth)

(now the ears of my ears awake and
now the eyes of my eyes are opened)
> —E E CUMMINGS, from
> Poem #65, in XAIPE
> collection

We began this book by speaking of death as a lost season, an unconfronted theme in our culture. We said that death must become better known to us if we are to illuminate the darker aspects of ourselves and the frightening possibilities of our culture in this nuclear age.

The subject of death is now beginning to receive

a great deal of attention; the evidence of this is visible in newsstands, bookstores, sermons, psychiatric concerns, and in ordinary conversation. And yet, death remains not only opaque but offensive; it is difficult to speak of "progress" in this area. When Freud began to think and write about the unthinkable theme in his time—sexuality—he was shunned and dismissed as an irresponsible crank. In thinking about human nature today, we take for granted the importance of sexual impulses that find expression throughout the life cycle. Our present unthinkable (really unfeelable) theme is the threat to human continuity that characterizes our historic period. It is this threat that makes death unthinkable.

Freud helped us to an appreciation of more than just sexuality. In showing the ways in which sexual themes are represented in dreams and fantasies, he demonstrated the richness of the human capacity to symbolize. We are capable of attaching sexual meaning to objects and events that are not sexual but that become symbols of our sexual experiences and aspirations.

We choose *death and the continuity of life* as the theme around which to build a psychohistorical understanding of man. But we do so with no less awareness of the human capacity to create rich symbolic meanings around basic biological facts. People are born, mature, give birth to children, grow old, and die. To speak of an unbroken chain of human life consisting of birth, growth, and death and extending backward and forward in time is therefore simply to express a biological fact. But it is a biological fact that assumes complex kinds of psychological meanings for human beings and human cultures.

Death and Rebirth

Perhaps the most universal religious symbolism is that of death and rebirth. This symbolism derives its power from its closeness both to biological fact and to human aspiration—the fact of human birth and death and the aspiration for continuous and renewed life. In the Jewish expectation of the Messiah who will come and renew the community, in Christ's promise "to make all things new," in the Hindu vision of release from the mundane cycle of endless reincarnations—the hope of a new birth is a universal image of great psychic force.

But the counterpart to the image of rebirth is that of death to one's old self. "He who finds his life will lose it" is the way Christ expressed this. In our terms we might say that the profoundest insight is attainable only by the survivor: he who has touched death in some bodily or psychic way and has himself remained alive.

The winter which makes possible spring, the dark of night followed by the light of day, the suffering which prepares the way for the deepest insight and the greatest ecstasy—these are images of death and rebirth that find universal cultural expression. They suggest a human quest for forms of integrity, movement, and connection that affirm life in the face of death.

Death and rebirth is a profoundly hopeful image but not one of easy or shallow optimism. It suggests a process of personal and cultural transformation based on the experience of "hitting rock bottom" or touching death in some literal or imagined way. It is an image of the survivor—one who has traveled into the land of death—as seer and prophet and healer. It is an image of a quest for real and authentic meaning

121

in the wake of destruction of inauthentic identities and false claims.

The image is of the survivor as creator: the one who has known disintegration, separation, and stasis now struggling to achieve a new formulation of self and world. This process may involve exploration, experimentation, and risk as the search for new forms leads in unanticipated directions. And the process certainly involves tension as one tries to find external forms (such as styles of work, learning, family, relation to friends) that fit with one's emerging inner sense of self.

The survivor seeks form—both inner psychological form and outer form of life. The modes of symbolic immortality (in their inner symbolic representation and external embodiment in cultural institutions) become the spheres of inner and outer re-creation, of personal and cultural rebirth. The goal is the creation of institutions in which we can live but which also live in us, institutions that energize us and provide a sense of who we are and what we might become.

The survivor is one for whom having known the end makes possible a new beginning—a beginning freshly unencumbered by the weight of the old and the dead. We have spoken of survivors of the atomic bomb over Hiroshima. For them, the task of reconstructing the city and their own lives was a torturous process. How to establish forms of continuity amid total disruption? How to affirm the imagery of life after having known holocaust? How to become more than *just* survivors?

These survivor tasks have not been easy. Rebirth has been sought in acts of witness to the hard truth of the nuclear age. This witness has sometimes taken the form of various kinds of political commitment and work in the international peace movement, and sometimes of silent tribute to the dead. But holocaust is no guarantee of rebirth; having known the end does not ensure that one will make a new beginning. When a new formulation of self and world is not attained (and is perhaps not attainable), life constricts; sensitivities dull and become numb. Such psychic numbing is itself a form of death, a partial death that protects one from a reality too hard to face and too chaotic to formulate.

The term "psychic numbing" describes the lives of many of the Hiroshima survivors. But it also describes much more. The whole age in which we live is one of vast numbing and desensitization. Numbing occurs when what is experienced cannot be adequately symbolized, formulated, and expressed in individual and communal activity. This symbolic gap, and the resulting numbing, is far more vivid and extreme for the Hiroshima survivors. But such a symbolic gap exists for us all.

We can see both processes—survivor numbing and rebirth—in the experience of the nuclear scientists who did the research to produce the atomic bomb. These men became survivors, too, of their own work and of the holocaust their work made possible. For some of them the consequence was a further retrenchment around a vision of salvation based on nuclear weapons; others took a kind of prophetic mission in warning the world of the vastly increased danger.

Much closer to us is the contemporary survivor experience of Vietnam veterans. These men have returned home from a tainted and unglorious war to a nation confused about its own commitment to the war and to the men who fought it. Those veterans who explore their own confusions and guilt go through the most agonizing kinds of self-doubt as they try to find a new ethic by which to live in the society that sent them to war. The veterans of the Vietnam war have much to teach us about our culture and ourselves. We sense in their words and in their experience something that must be faced. As survivors of that experience, they confront us with truth at its source. What they say can make us uneasy to the point of resentment, but their message can also be extraordinarily compelling.

We can see in the Vietnam veterans the same alternative survivor patterns—numbing for some and a struggle toward transformation in others—that we saw in the Hiroshima bomb victims and nuclear scientists. For some of the men, personal identity becomes constricted; for others the process of finding new modes of being means a complex process of personal change.

Why do some survivors persist in a numbed relationship to their death immersion while others struggle toward rebirth? There is no clear answer to this important but difficult question. The personality strengths which the survivor brings with him from early life are no doubt crucial for what happens. But vital, too, is the kind of support which the survivor finds as he begins to reconstruct himself and his world.

Some Vietnam veterans have formed small rap groups in which they can explore together the meaning of their war experience and offer mutual support as they begin to rebuild their lives. While they constitute a small minority of the entire body of Vietnam veterans, we shall discuss this group in detail because they have significance beyond their numbers, and because we have worked with them in rap groups and individual interviews. Many of these men are haunted with guilt and disturbing memories of brutal atrocities of which they were a part. They feel that the war brought out the worst parts of themselves, and they wish to get back in touch with the best, if indeed the best parts still exist. They want to be able to trust themselves and other people, to create intimate relationships with other men, women, and children; they seek meaningful work and new political beliefs.

The men press hard in their re-examination of themselves. Questions about their experience in the military lead to questions about their images of manliness. Many of the men speak of a kind of John Wayne identification, prevalent throughout American culture with which they were brought up. They wanted to be "real men": strong, tough, hard—a form of manhood accentuated in the military to the point of caricature. Later, in seeking to change themselves, they find the old models must first be critically explored. The John Wayne image, involving the suppression of feeling, softness, and vulnerability, becomes an impediment in the process of personal change. One veteran said, "I don't know why I feel sorry. John Wayne never felt sorry." As the men themselves put it, personal transformation meant "kicking the John Wayne thing" so that a new and more sensitive manliness could emerge.

We can understand the survivor task of these veterans better if we understand the nature of the war they fought. The Vietnam war has been a war without heroes. The unseen enemy blended into the Vietnamese population and became indistinguishable from those we wished to "defend." In this situation, the American GI found himself exploited and cheated in small and large ways by Vietnamese children and bar girls, who were themselves struggling to survive, and by an evasive enemy who would not reveal himself. Massive American technology made available every variety of plane, bomb, and tank. Combat was inseparable from atrocity, and, in the absence of clear victories, the only indicator of "progress" was a spurious and grotesque "body count."

The war has thus been perceived as absurd, ridiculous, totally without meaning. Only the danger has been real. Buddies get wounded and die. One's own life is always at stake. And for what?

Out of most wars there emerge songs which express the nobility of the effort and the worth of the sacrifices being demanded. For many of the Vietnam veterans, the song which has best captured what the war is about is the "I-Feel-Like-I'm-Fixin'-to-Die Rag" of Country Joe and the Fish, of which the opening lines were quoted in Chapter 1. This is a song of mockery, a song that mocks the value of a war that itself has mocked the value of life.

We spoke earlier of the relationship of death imagery to victimization: The victim is seen as less than human, tainted by death, and therefore killable. In the war in Vietnam, a poor country of nonwhite people, American technological power became its own justification for the slaughter of people who lack that technology. The problem has been that the power has not worked. And the failure has raised questions about both American technology and the "nonhuman" Vietnamese who managed to fight so well.

The veterans speak of their own recovery from the war as "becoming human again," a process that is dependent upon coming to recognize the humanity of the Vietnamese whom they have so brutalized. Americans in Vietnam have referred to the Vietnamese people as "gooks" or "dinks"—terms of disparagement roughly equal to the term "nigger" for black people here. Terms like these are dehumanizing; that is their function. But in the end, they dehumanize the victimizers as well as the victims. They serve to blunt the victimizers' capacity to identify with other people and to feel. Such emotional blunting is what we have been calling "numbing."

As veterans begin to recognize that the victims of their war activities have been human beings—that they have killed people like themselves—they actively open themselves to guilt. They begin to feel a sense of personal responsibility for what they have done. They struggle to balance this sense of personal responsibility with the awareness that the war thrust them into what may be called an "atrocity-producing situation." They come to value their guilt as central to their regained capacity to feel, and they develop an animating relationship to that guilt. For many, on the contrary, guilt is static and self-destructive, leading to various kinds of depression and related forms of mental disturbance. There are, however, vast numbers of veterans who remain at least partly numb with little indication of either guilt or insight.

Even those who examine their experience find that,

upon their return, their numbing did not suddenly lift. They remain suspicious of themselves and others, experience sudden outbursts of violent rage and fear, and have great difficulty establishing relationships of emotional closeness. They grope toward a way to express and give meaning to their experience. In this effort to give form to their feelings, they show the survivor's need to achieve a new sense of self and world. They take on the survivor mission of telling their tale, and they tell it with rare intensity and moral force. Their truth must be shared; others must be enabled to participate in their survivor experience and, above all, to share the guilt and responsibility. Telling the tale is a political act and involves the men with new colleagues in the antiwar movement, new assumptions and new activities.

The experience is not only "psychotherapy" in the sense of inner reflections and talk. The men look both inward and outward; they are both self-critical and critical of society. The transformation goes far beyond where it began: What they undertook as personal self-exploration broadens to involve a new relationship to the world. The transformation is, in short, "psychohistorical," just as the war itself had both psychological and historical dimensions.

Those who have known this small group of veterans we are describing feel them to possess, not only individually, but collectively as well, something approaching a prophetic quality. They have been to the far reaches of what this culture is capable of creating (a land of death), and they return with grim but potentially revitalizing truth. Their rebirth becomes a demand upon the rest of us.

The Vietnam war was a reflection of deeper conflicts in American society, but remains with us as a pervasive agony of its own. Like the veterans, but in vaguer and more amorphous ways, we are all survivors of Vietnam. Our survivor emotions blend with the smaller and more immediate agonies of our lives and, if well used, offer the possibility of new solutions. But again like the veterans, we must be content with the institutions and forms in our society and in ourselves that resist change or transformation. We share with the veterans alternatives of denial and destructiveness on the one hand and new beginnings on the other.

Both we and the veterans have available a psychological style which had been evolving in the United States and elsewhere long before the Vietnam war. This psychological style involves continual experimentation with new forms of belief and styles of life in an effort to reanimate one's self and one's world. The impulse toward self-evolution and experimentation in this psychological style derive from the psychohistorical dislocations of our time. They reflect both a hunger for the new, in all aspects of life, and a great mistrust of static forms. We call this style *Protean* after the Greek god Proteus, who had a gift for shape-shifting. Protean men and women are survivors of recent and more remote twentieth-century holocausts. But the search for new forms reflects a collapse of cultural values which has been occurring in the Western world for several centuries, and has become especially acute during the last few decades. The Protean style is most evident among the young, but it inhabits the old as well.

The creative possibilities of the Protean style are

reflected in the remarkable series of changes we see in many people's lives. But there are dangers too. The Protean style can represent a profound quest for new forms having ultimately to do with revitalizing the modes of immortality. But it can also deteriorate into a plastic style in which the stress is on superficial adaptation, fitting in and touching everything rather than making things new. Protean man or woman is a survivor of holocaust, of unprecedented historical velocity, and of the various dislocations of life and death that we have discussed. In its more generative versions, the Protean style confronts our sense of loss and our anxiety about death, but in its plastic versions, these feelings are avoided.

Another survivor reaction is *constriction,* or closing in. Here, to escape anxiety about death, the survivor avoids the possibilities of life and the existence of change. A constricted response of this sort involves taking a stand against alteration of the modes of immortality. The constricted person insists that social patterns remain adequate, but this insistence is, to a considerable degree, a reaction to the Protean style which is so widespread among us.

A constricted pattern is discernible in the condemnation of youth culture by those who are frightened of the possibilities of change, though the young themselves are hardly immune from such responses. The tension between the Protean and constricted styles sometimes underlies the generation gap, and may be even more fundamental than the generation gap itself. This whole issue raises a very basic question: How much personality constriction (and even numbing) is necessary as one assumes the responsibilities of adulthood? How much play can adulthood retain?

Adults, after all, must perform society's work—work that includes raising children, teaching the young, constructing cities, healing the sick, producing and purchasing food and clothing. All these tasks require various degrees of skill and professionalization. Can one be adult and Protean too? Many men and women are confronting that question today as they confront the sense of "living deadness" emanating from holocaust, rapid change, large impersonal bureaucratic structures, and the image of the machine. They seek new forms of connection, movement, and integrity around which to build new communities for living and working. To understand the experiments of survivor as creator and the process of reconstructing —resymbolizing—the community, we shall return to the five modes of immortality.

The *biological-biosocial mode* is at issue in the new kinds of families and family-like structures presently taking shape. These groups (sometimes, but not always, called communes) concern themselves with the most basic psychological and biological matters: organic food, greater sexual freedom, collective child rearing, spontaneity of mental and physical expression.

Closely related to these developments are altered conceptions of manhood and womanhood. We have seen how the Vietnam war has focused for many men the question of what it means to be a man. The veterans were able to connect with patterns of youth culture in which the American male ideal of the tough, tight-lipped, physically powerful, no-nonsense, highly competitive sexual conqueror has begun to give way to an image of a more gentle, open, "soft," physically unimpressive, artistically minded self-explorer. Important for such transformations are the models of maleness provided by Protean figures like Bob Dylan.

In the same way, the feminine ideal of the soft, self-sacrificing, family-oriented helpmate is being challenged by that of the aggressive, physically and emotionally strong, self-expanding, liberation-oriented feminist. Such experimentation in sexual identity has inevitably involved excesses and absurdities. But in exploring the center and the edges (wherever these may lie) of what we mean by maleness and femaleness, the society struggles with perhaps the most crucial psychological question of all.

Within the *theological or spiritual mode,* the Protean quest is evident in a wide range of religious explorations. Some embrace forms of religious commitment that stress social and political concern and activism. Others reject these concerns as "world-centered" and look instead for intense varieties of inner experience and meditation. Both the intensity and the variety of these explorations are striking, ranging as they do from that of Jesus freaks to various forms of Eastern and occult spirituality.

The most characteristic feature of much religious experimentation is what the Catholic theologian John Dunne calls "the new religion of our time": "a phenomenon we might call 'passing over,' . . . a going over to the standpoint of another culture, another way of life, another religion . . . followed by an equal and opposite process we might call 'coming back,' coming back with new insight to one's own culture, one's own way of life, one's own religion."

The Protean quest itself thus parallels a religious search, a form of "wandering" and looking for ever truer truths. The *process,* rather than being a once-and-for-all "passing over" and "coming back," may in fact be endless. As such, the religious impulse may become a continuous quest, whether involving many doctrines in turn or significant shifts within a single religious commitment.

We have spoken of the important transformation related to immortality via man's *works.* The questions being asked today about the nature of jobs and the meaning of work do not have only to do with making work pleasurable or eliminating work altogether. The basic theme is the quest for significant work experience that will be immediately involving and that will contribute to the continuing human enterprise.

What we call work is a vitally important boundary between one's evolving personality and one's social vision. Large numbers of men and women today are demanding greater harmony at that boundary. This means that one's job (work) must be comprehensible in terms of some contribution ("works") he hopes to make, and that the old vocation-avocation (work-play) division must be less mutually exclusive. Work communes (in which groups of teachers, lawyers, medical workers, artists, or political workers live together) are now appearing, as people who are engaged in the Protean quest search collectively and seek each other's support, within a family-like setting, for establishing their new patterns of work.

The quest for symbolic immortality via relationship to *nature* is reflected in a concern for a polluted, ugly, and deteriorating environment. There is also a continuing movement back to nature with city dwellers becoming backwoodsmen and farmers. It can, of course, appear quite absurd for young people to seek solutions to the problems of advanced industrial society by fleeing from New York and Chicago to the Vermont woods or the hills of California. But again we must not lose sight of what is most fundamentally involved. Particular rural communes may not last; their inhabitants may move on, may even return to the city. In all of this, however, there is experimentation with the self in which this contemporary form of return to nature can help to revitalize the imagination in ways that will eventually affect the whole society.

The rhythms of nature have always been a vital source of refreshment for the human imagination. It is interesting in fact that the terms we use to describe an impaired imagination—terms like "stagnated" or "wilted"—are metaphors taken from nature. Nature is a source of spiritual nurture ("symbolic reordering") as well as physical sustenance. In seeking a closer relationship to nature, the psychological significance of natural imagery is reaffirmed.

We have said that the final mode, *experiential transcendence,* is basic to the other four, but we can see it now to be equally basic to the experience of change itself. In this sense the "drug revolution" of the 1960's has had great significance in challenging existing modes of consciousness. More important than the drugs themselves has been the concern with consciousness and their contribution to developing new social and psychological forms.

Hence, we find people seeking varieties of experiential transcendence not only through drugs or meditation but in their work, politics, play, and everyday relationships. The issue is less that of dramatic public forms of ecstasy than of periodic or sustained experience of exquisite inner harmony, of wholeness and unity. For some people at the forefront of what might be called experiential radicalism, moments of transcendence—however induced —are self-justifying and are, in fact, the justification of everything else. For others, such moments lead to renewed life exploration and to new forms of commitment. Critics of experiential radicalism have disagreed about whether to view this mode as a valuable path to a "break-through" or as an "escape from reality." Indeed, these experiential forays can be a diversion and a retreat from the painful contradictions of a disorganized existence. But they can also yield the most vital kinds of symbolic reordering.

Experiential transcendence is a model for and a path toward an altered relationship to time and death. This is true either in establishing or altering one's mode of continuity, whether "living on" in one's children, works, spiritual state, or relationship to nature.

But these explorations cannot be free of pain and doubt. "In the worst night of my will/I dared to question all," writes the poet Theodore Roethke. And elsewhere he writes, "Caught in the dying light/I thought myself reborn." The imagery of rebirth, of deep and profound transformation, is the counterpart of the imagery of death. In turning away from the one, we inevitably exclude the other.

The ancient principle of death and rebirth affects all our enterprises; every significant step in human experience involves some inner sense of death. The image of rebirth is inseparable from hope itself. The holocausts of our time and our own Protean possibilities call forth that image in us. Again, Roethke:

> In a dark time,
> The eye begins to see.

Suggestions for Further Reading

AGEE, JAMES. *A Death in the Family.* New York: Grosset & Dunlap, 1938; London: Peter Owen, 1971.

ANTHONY, SYLVIA. *The Discovery of Death in Childhood and After.* London: Allen Lane, 1971; New York: Basic Books, 1972.

BEAUVOIR, SIMONE DE. *A Very Easy Death.* New York: G. P. Putnam's Sons, 1966; London: Andre Deutsch and Weidenfeld & Nicolson, 1966.

BECKER, ERNST. *The Denial of Death.* New York: The Free Press, 1973.

BOWLBY, JOHN. *Separation: Anxiety and Anger.* Vol. 2: *Attachment and Loss.* New York: Basic Books, 1973; London: Tavistock, 1973.

BRANDON, S. G. F. *The Judgment of the Dead: The Idea of Life After Death in the Major Religions.* New York: Charles Scribner's Sons, 1967; London: Weidenfeld & Nicolson, 1967.

BROWN, NORMAN O. *Life Against Death: The Psychoanalytical Meaning of History.* New York: Vintage, 1959; London: Routledge, 1959.

CHORON, JACQUES. *Modern Man and Mortality.* New York: Macmillan, 1963.

COTTLE, THOMAS J. "The Connections of Adolescence." *Daedalus* 100, no. 4 (Fall 1971).

DUNNE, JOHN S. *The City of the Gods: A Study in Myth and Mortality.* New York: Macmillan, 1965.

———. *Time and Myth: A Meditation on Storytelling as*

an Exploration of Life and Death. Garden City, N.Y.: Doubleday, 1973.

FEIFEL, HERMAN, editor. *The Meaning of Death.* New York: McGraw-Hill, 1959.

FREUD, SIGMUND. *Beyond the Pleasure Principle* (1920). New York: Bantam, 1959; London: Hogarth, 1961.

———. "Reflections upon War and Death" (1915), "On Transience" (1916), in PHILIP RIEFF, editor, *Sigmund Freud: Character and Culture.* New York: Collier, 1963.

FULTON, ROBERT. *Death and Identity.* New York and Chichester, Eng.: John Wiley & Sons, 1965.

GEORGE, PETER. *Dr. Strangelove; or, How I Learned to Stop Worrying and Love the Bomb.* London: Corgi, 1970; New York: Bantam, 1972.

GLASER, BARNEY G. and ANSELM L. STRAUSS. *Awareness of Dying.* Chicago: Aldine, 1965; London: Weidenfeld & Nicolson, 1966.

GORER, GEOFFREY. *Death, Grief and Mourning.* Garden City, N.Y.: Doubleday, 1965; London: Cresset, 1965.

———. "The Pornography of Death," in MAURICE R. STEIN, ARTHUR J. VIDICH, and DAVID MANNING WHITE, editors, *Identity and Anxiety.* Glencoe, Ill.: Free Press, 1960; London: Collier-Macmillan, 1963.

JUNG, CARL. *Modern Man in Search of a Soul.* New York: Harcourt, Brace & World, 1933; London: Routledge, 1933.

———. "On Life After Death," in *Memories, Dreams, Reflections.* New York: Pantheon, 1962; London: Routledge & Collins, 1963.

KAPLEAU, PHILIP, editor. *The Wheel of Death: A Collection of Writings from Zen Buddhist and Other Sources on Dying–Death–Rebirth.* New York: Harper & Row, 1971; London: Allen and Unwin, 1972.

KASTENBAUM, ROBERT, and RUTH AISENBERG. *The Psychology of Death.* New York: Springer, 1972.

KUBLER-ROSS, ELISABETH. *On Death and Dying.* New York: Macmillan, 1970.

LEWIS, C. S. *A Grief Observed.* Greenwich, Conn.: Seabury, 1961; London: Faber & Faber, 1961.

LIFTON, ROBERT JAY. *Boundaries: Psychological Man in Revolution.* New York: Random House, 1970.

——. *Death in Life: Survivors of Hiroshima.* New York: Random House, 1967; London: Weidenfeld & Nicolson, 1968.

——. *Home from the War: Vietnam Veterans—Neither Victims nor Executioners.* New York: Simon & Schuster, 1973; London: Wildwood House, 1974.

——. *Revolutionary Immortality: Mao Tse-tung and the Chinese Cultural Revolution.* New York: Random House, 1967; London: Weidenfeld & Nicolson, 1969.

MITFORD, JESSICA. *The American Way of Death.* New York: Simon & Schuster, 1963; London: Hutchinson, 1963.

PARKES, COLIN MURRAY. *Bereavement: Studies of Grief in Adult Life.* New York: International Universities Press, 1972; London: Tavistock, 1972.

RANK, OTTO. *Beyond Psychology.* New York: Dover, 1941.

SHNEIDMAN, EDWIN S. *Deaths of Man.* New York: Quadrangle Press, 1973.

STENDAHL, KRISTER, editor. *Immortality and Resurrection—Death in the Western World: Two Conflicting Currents of Thought.* New York: Macmillan, 1965.

TILLICH, PAUL. "The Eternal Now," in *The Eternal Now.* New York: Charles Scribner's Sons, 1963; London: S.C.M.P., 1967.

TOLSTOY, LEO. "The Death of Ivan Ilych," in *The Death of Ivan Ilych and Other Stories.* New York: New American Library, 1960.

WAUGH, EVELYN. *The Loved One.* New York: Dell, 1948; London: Chapman & Hall, 1965.

WEISMAN, AVERY D. *On Dying and Denying: A Psychiatric Study of Terminality.* New York: Behavioral Publications, 1972.

WOODWARD, KENNETH L. "How America Lives with Death." *Newsweek,* April 6, 1970, pp. 81–88.

Index

ABOUT THE AUTHORS

ROBERT JAY LIFTON holds the Foundations' Fund for Research in Psychiatry professorship at Yale University. His books include *Home from the War; Death in Life: Survivors of Hiroshima* (winner of the National Book Award and the Van Wyck Book Award in 1969); and *History and Human Survival*. A cartoonist by avocation, he has published a book of humorous cartoons, entitled *Birds*.

ERIC OLSON is a graduate student in psychology at Harvard University and has taught at a number of colleges and schools in the United States and India. He and Robert Lifton are currently studying the Protean style in young adulthood and psychological responses following disaster, and are editing a book of papers on psychohistory.

INTIMATE REFLECTIONS

Thoughts, ideas, and perceptions of life as it is.

- [ ] THE LIVES OF A CELL: NOTES OF A BIOLOGY WATCHER Lewis Thomas 6303 • $1.75
- [ ] LIVING AND DYING Robert Jay Lifton and Eric Olson 6347 • $1.95
- [ ] THE SAVAGE GOD A. Alvarez 7580 • $1.95
- [ ] RICHIE Thomas Thompson 8327 • $1.50
- [ ] PILGRIM AT TINKER CREEK Annie Dillard 8700 • $1.95
- [ ] ELLEN: A SHORT LIFE, LONG REMEMBERED Rose Levit 8729 • $1.25
- [ ] WIDOW Lynn Caine 8766 • $1.75
- [ ] THOMAS JEFFERSON: AN INTIMATE HISTORY Fawn Brodie 8787 • $2.50
- [ ] GATHER TOGETHER IN MY NAME Maya Angelou 8801 • $1.50
- [ ] AMERICAN ODYSSEY Robert Conot 8860 • $2.95
- [ ] ZEN AND THE ART OF MOTORCYCLE MAINTENANCE Robert M. Pirsig 8880 • $2.25

Buy them at your local bookstore or use this handy coupon for ordering:

Bantam Books, Inc., Dept. EDR, 414 East Golf Road, Des Plaines, IL 60016

Please send me the books I have checked above. I am enclosing
$_____(please add 35¢ to cover postage and handling).
Send check or money order—no cash or C.O.D.'s please.

Mr/Mrs/Miss_____

Address_____

City_____State/Zip_____

EDR—12/75

Please allow three weeks for delivery. This offer expires 12/76.